MEMORABLE WALKS IN SAN FRANCISCO

WITHDRAWN

6th Edition

Wiley Publishing, Inc.

Published by:

WILEY PUBLISHING, INC.

111 River St.
Hoboken, NJ 07030-5774

ISBN-13: 978-0-471-77340-5
ISBN-10: 0-471-77340-9

Editor: Jennifer Moore
Production Editor: Lindsay Thompson
Photo Editor: Richard Fox
Cartographer: Elizabeth Puhl
Production by Wiley Indianapolis Composition Services

For information on our other products and services or to obtain techni-
cal support, please contact our Customer Care Department within the
U.S. at 800/762-2974, outside the U.S. at 317/572-3993 or fax
317/572-4002.

Wiley also publishes its books in a variety of electronic formats. Some
content that appears in print may not be available in electronic formats.

Manufactured in the United States of America

5   4   3   2   1

Contents

LIST OF MAPS

The Walking Tours

• • • • • • • • • • • • • • • • •

About the Author

Native San Franciscan **Erika Lenkert** fled the dot-community to find respite and great food and wine in Napa Valley. When she's not writing about food, wine, and travel for the likes of *Four Seasons Magazine* or *InStyle,* or promoting her book *The Last-Minute Party Girl: Fashionable, Fearless, and Foolishly Simple Entertaining,* she's in search of Wine Country pleasures to share with Frommer's readers. She also remains subservient to her owners—two Siamese cats and most recently, her new daughter Viva.

In addition to this guide, Erika authors and co-authors a number of other Frommer's guides to California, including *Frommer's California* and *Frommer's San Francisco.*

Acknowledgments

Erika would like to thank Lyla Max for not only tirelessly pouring over these pages to help confirm their accuracy, but also for providing excellent newborn advice, reassurance, and friendship—free of charge.

An Invitation to the Reader

In researching this book, we discovered many wonderful places—hotels, restaurants, shops, and more. We're sure you'll find others. Please tell us about them, so we can share the information with your fellow travelers in upcoming editions. If you were disappointed with a recommendation, we'd love to know that, too. Please write to:

Frommer's Memorable Walks in San Francisco, 6th Edition
Wiley Publishing, Inc.
111 River St. • Hoboken, NJ 07030-5774

An Additional Note

Please be advised that travel information is subject to change at any time—and this is especially true of prices. We therefore suggest that you write or call ahead for confirmation when making your travel plans. The authors, editors, and publisher cannot be held responsible for the experiences of readers while traveling. Your safety is important to us, however, so we encourage you to stay alert and be aware of your surroundings. Keep a close eye on cameras, purses, and wallets, all favorite targets of thieves and pickpockets.

Frommers.com

Now that you have the guidebook to a great trip, visit our website at **www.frommers.com** for travel information on more than 3,000 destinations. With features updated regularly, we give you instant access to the most current trip-planning information available. At Frommers.com, you'll also find the best prices on airfares, accommodations, and car rentals—and you can even book travel online through our travel booking partners. At Frommers.com, you'll also find the following:

- Online updates to our most popular guidebooks
- Vacation sweepstakes and contest giveaways
- Newsletter highlighting the hottest travel trends
- Online travel message boards with featured travel discussions

Introducing
San Francisco

There are some cities that are best seen on foot, and San Francisco is one of them. Unlike burgeoning metropolises such as Los Angeles, whose boundless sprawl blurs the line between city and suburbia, San Francisco is confined by bay and sea to a mere 47 square miles of highly coveted real estate.

The result, not surprisingly, is an incredibly dense concentration of interesting culture, architecture, food, and urban life. Americans may think big as a whole, but most San Franciscans are content to coexist in crowded—and dearly priced—confines, a small price to pay (so we say) for living in one of the world's most popular cities.

There are few places on earth where one can find so much to do, see, eat, and enjoy within such a condensed and readily walkable radius. Truth is, San Francisco is one big, beautiful walking tour; all I've done is broken it down into manageable parts, added a dash of historical lore and a pinch of modern-day gossip, and packaged each tour into a thoroughly enjoyable 2- to 3-hour jaunt through the city's past lives and present virtues.

The Tours at a Glance

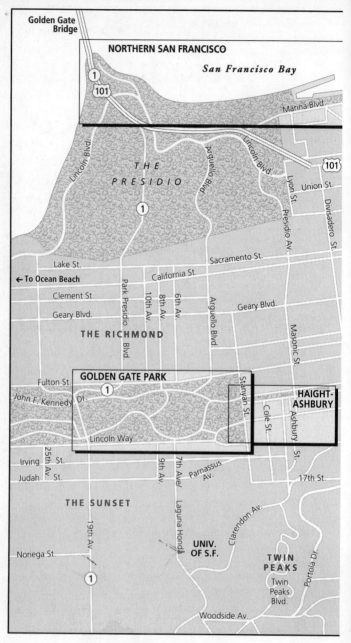

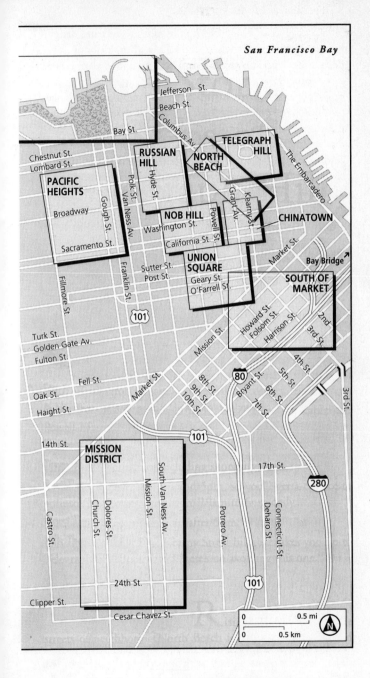

San Francisco Bay

Jefferson St.
Beach St.
Bay St.

Chestnut St.
Lombard St.

PACIFIC HEIGHTS

Broadway

Sacramento St.

RUSSIAN HILL

NORTH BEACH

TELEGRAPH HILL

NOB HILL

Washington St.
California St.

CHINATOWN

UNION SQUARE

Geary St.
O'Farrell St.

Sutter St.
Post St.

Market St.

Bay Bridge

SOUTH OF MARKET

Howard St.
Folsom St.
Harrison St.

Turk St.
Golden Gate Av.
Fulton St.

Fell St.

Oak St.
Haight St.

14th St.

MISSION DISTRICT

17th St.

24th St.

Clipper St.
Cesar Chavez St.

Gough St.
Van Ness Av.
Polk St.
Hyde St.
Franklin St.
Fillmore St.
Columbus Av.
Grant Av.
Kearny St.
Powell St.
The Embarcadero
Mission St.
Market St.
8th St.
9th St.
10th St.
Bryant St.
5th St.
6th St.
7th St.
2nd St.
3rd St.
4th St.
3rd St.
17th St.
South Van Ness Av.
Mission St.
Dolores St.
Church St.
Castro St.
Potrero Av.
Connecticut St.
Deharo St.

101

80

101

280

0   0.5 mi
0   0.5 km

N

I continue to be amazed by the sultry secrets and delightful wonders San Francisco conceals within its boundaries. Each time I update this book, I am reminded that around every corner lies yet another enticing shop, grand old mansion, or little-known historical tidbit that has long been overlooked or unknown, even by residents. It's the little things that count the most: an intricately carved medallion on a Victorian frieze, that weathered wooden stairway leading into a river of small gardens, the modest abode of Robert Louis Stevenson—little things that add to my growing appreciation for one of the most intriguing cities on earth.

Of course, I'm biased because I live here. But I'm also absolutely certain that you will enjoy these walking tours, regardless of your age or agility. Whether you're into Edwardian homes or roller-disco, there's a walking tour here for you. All you need to do is don your walking shoes and find out for yourself why San Franciscans are forever smitten by our City by the Bay.

THE TOURS AT A GLANCE

Walk 1: Union Square Past & Present

There's no better way to indulge in San Francisco's metropolitan culture than to begin at Union Square. Here, not only can you do enough department-store shopping to max out all your credit cards, but you can also stroll through a notorious late-nineteenth-century red-light district, catch a bird's-eye view from a high-rise, and see the effect that the devastating 1906 earthquake had on some of San Francisco's most famous downtown landmarks.

Walk 2: Chinatown: History, Culture, Dim Sum & Then Some

An exotic afternoon awaits you within the maze of small, crowded streets that make up Chinatown. Here, you can taste dim sum delicacies you can't pronounce (let alone identify), join locals in herb and tea shops, and set foot on the exact spot where the American flag was raised and gold-rush fever began.

Walk 3: Getting to Know North Beach

The pleasures of eating well, with an occasional sidebar or two of historical interest interjected for good measure, make up the theme of this waddle. Food, food, and more food—washed down with copious quantities of good coffee, beer, and wine—forms its centerpiece. All that's required of you is an appetite.

Walk 4: The Storied Steps of Telegraph Hill

San Francisco is a city of stairs, and no other walk is replete with so many steps—both up and down—as this one. It starts with a little shopping on Grant Street in North Beach, then winds its way up to Coit Tower and back down to sea level by way of the famed Filbert Steps. If you like lofty views, quaint gardens, and firm calves, this one's for you.

Walk 5: The Haughty Hotels of Nob Hill

History buffs, hotel hounds, and gearheads will love this one, which begins in high style at the top of Nob Hill and winds its way through some of San Francisco's finest hotels, past a trio of gorgeous homes, finally ending at the riveting Cable Car Museum.

Walk 6: The Ghosts of Russian Hill

San Francisco has always been a haven for writers, poets, and architects, many of whom resided on the steep slopes of Russian Hill. Literary history, scenery, and serenity pervade this walk, which is a must for both American-literature buffs and fans of the architect Willis Polk.

Walk 7: The Majestic Homes of Pacific Heights

If your dream house isn't among the grand facades you'll pass on this Pacific Heights tour, maybe there's something wrong with you! Seriously, though, the tall tales of who lived where and who killed whom in this neighborhood are just as compelling as the over-the-top architecture. And if you like to shop, you'll love the finale.

Walk 8: South of Market: A Civilized Afternoon of Arts & Leisure

Only recently has South of Market become the area of choice for a civilized and culturally stimulating afternoon. But with the Museum of Modern Art and the Yerba Buena Gardens within a few blocks of one another, you can't but walk away feeling inspired.

Walk 9: The Culture & Color of the Mission District

A trip south of the border without catching a flight? You betcha. Just follow me on this tour, where brightly painted murals, Latin music, food, culture, and the oldest building in the city await.

Walk 10: A Historical Flashback
Through Haight-Ashbury

Sure, there's still plenty of tie-dye and lost youth to commemorate the past in the renowned and colorful Haight-Ashbury district. But the remnants of this neighborhood's '60s counterculture movement are easy to miss if you don't know where to look. This walk takes you to the house where The Grateful Dead lived and played in the '60s, pauses for a historical flashback or two, leads you to some great cheap-food noshes, and shows you where to buy retro paraphernalia. It's a colorful visit to an only-in-San-Francisco scene.

Walk 11: Golden Gate Park: A Museum,
Blooms & Trees from Dunes

This Golden Gate Park tour offers an intimate introduction to what, in my mind, is the most beautiful, diverse, and entertaining 3½-mile-long patch of grass in the world. Between stops to smell the flowers, you'll encounter an extensive collection of Asian art, penguins, and crocodiles, as well as a great gilded Buddha. All that, and plenty of room to toss around a Frisbee—what more could you ask for?

Walk 12: The Golden Gate

As far as views go, there's nothing more magical than hoofing it along the city's northern shore, where ogle-worthy ocean and bay panoramas are backed by exclusive homes, bustling marinas, and pristine nature preserves.

Union Square Past & Present

Start: Union Square, bounded by Powell, Post, Stockton, and Geary streets.

Public Transportation: Bus: 2, 3, 4, 30, 38, 45, or 76; cable cars: Powell-Hyde or Powell-Mason; Metro (Powell Station): F, J, K, L, M, or N; BART.

Finish: Market and Fifth streets (Hallidie Plaza).

Time: 2 hours.

Best Times: Monday through Saturday between 10am and 6pm.

Worst Times: Nighttime; major holidays when shops are closed.

Hills That Could Kill: None.

It seems as if almost all buses—and credit-card bills—lead to the area known as "Union Square," the epicenter of San Francisco shopping, theater, and tourist culture. But tucked among the large hotels, restaurants, and department stores are dozens of interesting sights, many of which are unknown even to the local populace.

This area is steeped in colorful history, so along with your fill of sightseeing and serious shopping and dining destinations, you can also get a glimpse into bygone San Francisco. By the end of this tour, you'll be more in sync with the city's essence than the thousands of surrounding tourists who move like cattle toward yet another national department-store chain.

• • • • • • • • • • • • • • • •

Our tour begins at:

1. **Union Square,** located just north of Market Street and bounded by Powell, Post, Geary, and Stockton streets. Union Square was so named because it was here that meetings were held in support of the Union during the Civil War. In the 1960s the flower children came, hoping to enlighten and recruit new members for their antiwar movement. It also was here that a gay activist group, the Sisters of Perpetual Indulgence, organized in 1987 to protest the visit of Pope John Paul II.

   Today's Union Square looks nothing like it did in the past—in fact, it doesn't even look the same as did a few years ago. That's because of a major renovation that took place in 2002. This makeover transformed the center of the square, previously preferred by the homeless, into a glossy, welcoming courtyard with terraced grass areas, sculpture, a 360-degree view of surrounding shops such as Victoria's Secret, Tiffany & Co., Saks, The Disney Store, Macy's, and Levi's, and plenty of spots for sitting, sunning, and speculating. What remains from the old square is its trademark 90-foot granite shaft with a bronze statue called *Victory.* The model for the statue was the famous San Franciscan socialite Mrs. Adolph de Bretteville. It was erected in celebration of Admiral Dewey's victory at Manila Bay during the Spanish-American War, and was dedicated by Theodore Roosevelt in 1903.

   In recent years a consortium of artists has displayed artwork for sale here. These local talents are members of the Artists Guild of San Francisco, who are juried before they may join the group.

Union Square

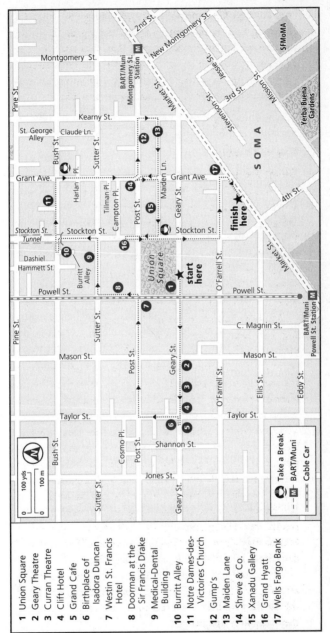

Map labels (as shown):

Montgomery St.

2nd St.

New Montgomery St.

SFMoMA

Pine St.

BART/Muni Montgomery St. Station

Market St.

3rd St.

Mission St.

Jessie St.

Stevenson St.

Yerba Buena Gardens

Kearny St.

St. George Alley

Claude Ln.

Bush St.

Sutter St.

S O M A

13

12

Grant Ave.

Harlan

Tillman Pl.

Campton Pl.

Maiden Ln.

Post St.

Geary St.

Grant Ave.

17

14

11

15

Stockton St. Tunnel

Stockton St.

Stockton St.

16

finish here ★

4th St.

Dashiel Hammett St.

10

9

Burritt Alley

Union Square

O'Farrell St.

Market St.

Powell St.

8

start here ★

1

Powell St.

7

BART/Muni Powell St. Station

C. Magnin St.

Pine St.

Mason St.

Post St.

Geary St.

2

Mason St.

O'Farrell St.

Ellis St.

Eddy St.

Taylor St.

3

4

Taylor St.

Cosmo Pl.

Post St.

6

5

Shannon St.

Bush St.

N

0   100 yds

0   100 m

Sutter St.

Geary St.

Jones St.

Take a Break

BART/Muni

Cable Car

Legend:

1 Union Square
2 Geary Theatre
3 Curran Theatre
4 Clift Hotel
5 Grand Cafe
6 Birthplace of Isadora Duncan
7 Westin St. Francis Hotel
8 Doorman at the Sir Francis Drake
9 Medical-Dental Building
10 Burritt Alley
11 Notre Dames-des-Victoires Church
12 Gump's
13 Maiden Lane
14 Shreve & Co.
15 Xanadu Gallery
16 Grand Hyatt
17 Wells Fargo Bank

That's about it for Union Square itself. Generally, this is just a place to stop and get your bearings before venturing through the downtown streets. If you do shop, though, leave your selections on hold at each store until the end of this tour. Lugging them around would prove to be intolerable.

Head to the right (west) on Geary Street, looking across the street for 415 Geary St., the:

2. **Geary Theater.** After the 1906 earthquake and fire gutted all eight of San Francisco's downtown performance theaters (along with almost everything else), the city wasted no time creating new homes for the performing arts. Within 5 years of the quake, eight new buildings had been constructed, and the majestic Geary Theater was one of them. Of those, the Geary, built in 1909, was the only one still continually operating as a full-time professional theater in 1989, when another earthquake again set the stage for change.

On October 17, 1989, less than 2 hours before ushers would begin seating theatergoers, the Loma Prieta quake sent a serious shakedown through the building. Its proscenium arch collapsed, ripping a 2,000-square-foot hole in the ceiling and sending tons of debris into the first six rows of orchestra seating. No one was injured, but the theater closed for 6 years and underwent a $29-million renovation and seismic reinforcement.

Today the historic Geary stands in all its restored glory. All the architectural nuances of original architects Walter D. Bliss and William B. Faville (who also designed the city's St. Francis Hotel) remain. Its exterior reflects the late-Victorian tradition of combining neoclassicism with a baroque influence, as does the respectfully renovated interior. As the permanent home to the American Conservatory Theater, the 1,024-seat hall regularly hosts world-renowned performances.

Also across the street, but a bit farther along, at 445 Geary St., you'll see the:

3. **Curran Theatre,** built in 1922 of reinforced concrete. This is one of the city's main theaters and is noteworthy

for its mansard roof and metal sign frames. This is the main theater for the Best of Broadway series. Take note that if you do buy tickets to see a show here, make sure you don't get stuck too far back in the balconies—the acoustics are poor.

Now cross to the side of Geary on which the theaters are located and head west toward Taylor Street. On your left, at the corner of Geary and Taylor streets, is the majestic:

4. **Clift Hotel,** at 495 Geary. Built just before the Panama Pacific International Exposition in 1915 for lawyer Frederick Clift (who had a suite designed especially for himself), this hotel was one of San Francisco's most elegant and beloved. Over the past decade it has been tossed from one management company to another, lost its luster, and landed in the hands of "hip hotelier" Ian Schrager, who thoroughly modernized its formerly old-world aura during a much-needed renovation. However, you can get a peek at the old-world grandeur in the renovated Redwood Room, the preferred downtown watering hole for the tragically hip. Appropriately named, this Art Deco room, which debuted in 1934, is paneled with the wood of a single, 2,000-year-old redwood tree and ornamented with gorgeous Deco sconces. If only they'd bring back the old bartenders and piano-bar vibe.

Return to the corner of Geary and Taylor streets and cross Taylor. On the southwest corner of Geary and Taylor at 501 Geary you'll find one of my favorite downtown dining options:

5. **Grand Cafe.** Even if you're not interested in where to have a great French-inspired California-cuisine lunch or dinner, it's worth taking a gander at San Francisco's grandest dining room. Step back beyond the front room's bar and "Petit Café" to scope out the enormous and truly stunning turn-of-the-20th-century ballroom–like dining oasis, which is a magnificent combination of old Europe and Art Nouveau, complete with playful sculptures, murals, and a cadre of dazzling Deco chandeliers. Since Chef Fabrice Roux took over the kitchen in 2005, it

Herb Caen

During his career as columnist for the *San Francisco Chronicle,* Herb Caen—the undisputed guru of three-dot journalism—covered the San Francisco scene for nearly 6 decades, contributing more than 16,000 columns with nary a missed beat. He witnessed and wrote about the city's evolution, from the construction of the Golden Gate Bridge to the dedication of the new Embarcadero promenade that bears his name. He reveled in the city, frequenting its social events, bashing its slovenly dressed, haranguing its politicians, and relating it all with a wink and a nod to the multitude of readers who devoured his column religiously each workday morning.

Along with his reflections on past and current events, Caen also added news bits sent in from readers to his daily column. For San Franciscans, it was a great feat to have their stories or establishments mentioned in one of his columns, a chance to bask in 15 minutes of unadulterated fame. A few of my friends were lucky enough to make the cut over the years, their tales told in classic Caen fashion:

Monday, August 30, 1993: "The Beat Goes On: Gordon Levinson, an accomplished drummer, has moved back to S.F. after a long absence to attend U.S.F. law school. Having no space to rehearse, he hauled his rig out to the Sloat end of Ocean Beach a few days ago. Wearing a Walkman headset, he was working on his tom-toms when a car raced up and out stepped a woman who tapped him

really is worth considering dining here. The humble French chef, who worked under previous bosses here for the past 5 years, is a star in the making. One bite of his deconstructed cassoulet (duck confit, baby back ribs, and turkey-artichoke sausage perched atop white beans in a delicate tomato sauce) will prove my point.

on the shoulder and said 'Sorry to interrupt—my name is Mary Kerr and I'm the gorilla keeper at the zoo across the street. Your drumming is sending our three male gorillas into an aggressive frenzy—they think they are about to be attacked—so would you mind?' Gordon packed up and moved on."

Tuesday, August 30, 1994: "Sarah Klein of the Fourth Ave. Kleins, who likes to blow bubbles with her squeezable bubble bear during slow traffic on the Bay Bridge, was pulled over, fergawdsake, by a Highway Patrolman who intoned, 'Only plain water and chicken feathers may be set free from a moving vehicle.' 'I don't have any chicken feathers,' said Sarah, rolling her eyes, but he was right: That's the section 23114-A of the Motor Vehicle Code, word for word, except that it's 'clear water and bird feathers,' ya turkey . . . The officer didn't give Sarah a ticket, confirming your suspicion that the real reason he pulled her over is that she's a looker."

But in early 1997, Herb's legacy of "raising Caen" came to an end. The man who unswervingly lived and loved San Francisco like no other died in February after a whirlwind of a year: He had won a Pulitzer Prize (or "Pullet Surprise" as he called it), married his longtime sweetheart, turned 80, and been diagnosed with inoperable cancer. He was never a rich man, but he parted this world with something no one can buy: the admiration and respect of a city that loved him as much as he loved it.

Once you've gotten your fill (and perhaps stopped for a bite or made a reservation) return to the corner of Geary and Taylor. Cross Geary to 501 Taylor St.:

6. **Birthplace of Isadora Duncan.** Duncan (1878–1927) was one of the most celebrated and innovative dancers of the early 20th century, and her origins here are noted by a plaque near the entrance of the building.

Isadora quit school at the age of 10 to study dance, and as a teen opened a dance school in San Francisco with her sister. The girls began teaching their "new system," which was based on natural and improvisational movements that attempted to interpret music and poetry.

Isadora soon grew tired of teaching, and was able to convince her mother to take her on tour with the little money they had managed to save. Duncan's first dance recitals in this country were not well received. But when she took her modern, free-spirited, freeform dance to London, she was "discovered" by Mrs. Patrick Campbell, who introduced Duncan to high-society London, as well as British royalty. It wasn't long before Duncan was adored all over Europe, known as the first woman to dance barefoot on stage. She also was the first person to perform interpretive dance to the music of the great composers. Ultimately her fame brought her back to San Francisco to perform at the Geary Theater.

Almost as renowned as her life was her tragic death. Duncan died in 1927 in Nice, France, in a freak accident—while driving, her trademark long red scarf became entangled in the wheel of her Bugatti sports car; she was strangled to death.

Continue along Taylor Street to the corner of Post Street. Cross Taylor and head east (right) down the south side of Post. Cross Mason, and when you come to the southwest corner of Post and Powell, go right. On your right, at 335 Powell, enter the impressive:

7. **Westin St. Francis Hotel.** During the late 19th century, Charles T. Crocker and a few of his wealthy buddies decided that San Francisco needed a world-class hotel, and so in 1904 up went the St. Francis. Only the latest technology was used in its construction, including a system of pipes that carried water directly from the ocean into the hotel's Turkish baths. Inside, service was state-of-the-art, too; some say the St. Francis was the first San Francisco hotel to use sheets on its beds. Since then, hordes of VIPs have hung their hats and hosiery here, including Emperor Hirohito, Queen Elizabeth II, Mother Teresa, King Juan Carlos of Spain, the Shah of Iran, and

all the U.S. presidents since Taft—except for George W. Bush, who hasn't made his way to our fair city since taking office. It's been a place for gossip, too: In 1921, Virginia Rappe's death here began the Fatty Arbuckle scandal that ended his career. Dashiell Hammett, while working for Pinkerton, was seen gathering evidence for Arbuckle's counsel in this very lobby. This also is where Gerald Ford escaped would-be-assassin Sara Jane Moore's bullet in 1975.

Like most downtown buildings, the city's second-oldest hotel was badly damaged during the earthquake and fire of 1906, but out of disaster came triumph; its reconstruction included an expansion that made the hotel the largest on the West Coast at that time.

Today, the St. Francis in many ways embodies San Francisco's finest, past and present. Stroll through the vast, ornate lobby and you can feel 100 years of history resonating from its hand-carved redwood paneling. Stop by the lobby's charm shop as visitors have done for more than 50 years (the thousands of silver, gold, and jewel-studded charms range from $12–$2,000 apiece). Ride the glass elevators in the back by the concierge for timeless and cheap thrills. For a memorable event that is anything but cheap, consider booking dinner here—the hotel is home to San Francisco's hottest and latest fine-dining restaurant, Michael Mina. Named after its owner/chef who became a top toque while overseeing the city's Aqua restaurant, this sexy fine-dining hot spot takes the small-plate dining concept to extremes with a three-course dinner that defies description. Suffice it to say that each course arrives as a trio of different renditions of the same theme—perhaps scallops or pork (plus three sides to match!) on custom Mina-designed modular china. That's six different preparations per dish, or a total of 18 different flavors over the course of an evening! It's a bit fussy for anyone who prefers to order a few things that sound good and eat lots of bites of them. But if the idea of sampling lots of styles and flavors appeal you, this edible food-combination case study is likely to be a culinary wonder.

Exit the hotel the same way you entered and backtrack toward Post Street. Cross both Post and Powell streets and continue north on Powell. Stop in front of the:

8. **Doorman at the Sir Francis Drake,** 450 Powell. It's an obscure fact, for sure, but it's interesting to note that Tom Sweeny, the head doorman, is a living historical monument. Dressed in traditional Beefeater attire (you can't miss those $1,400 duds), he's been the subject of countless snapshots for more than 20 years—an average of 200 per day—and has shaken hands with every president since Gerald Ford—including George W. Bush, but that happened in another city.

You also might want to return to this historic 1928 hotel in the evening to visit Harry Denton's Starlight Room. Its location at the top floor of the hotel (21 stories up), combined with the elegant 1930s scene, makes this one of the best places to catch the sunset or check out the nighttime skyline.

Continue to the corner of Sutter Street, cross it, and turn right, heading east on Sutter. Halfway down the block you will be standing in front of 450 Sutter, which is the:

9. **Medical-Dental Building,** which makes even a visit to the doctor mildly enjoyable. Designed by Timothy Pflueger and built in 1929, this towering steel-framed, terra-cotta–clad Art Deco building is striking even to those who couldn't care less about architecture. The entrance and the window frames are elaborately ornamented with Mayan relief work, the lobby and cast-aluminum ceiling are similarly gilded, and the ornate elevator doors beckon visitors to ride up to the doctors' offices. When entering the building, be sure to try the door at the farthest right. Because not all the front doors open, many visitors mistake the building for being closed.

Continue along Sutter Street to Stockton Street. Go left on Stockton, and at the end of the block, take the stairs—San Francisco's own little piece of New York City in the summertime. What do I mean? You need only take one whiff of the air and your nose will tell you.

At the top of the stairs, go left on Bush to:

10. **Burritt Alley.** Keep an eye out for the street sign, as it's blocked by a tree. Yes, it's nothing but a dirty alley with a patinated commemorative plaque, but Dashiell Hammett fans get a kick out of seeing this infamous spot where Hammett's fictional character Miles Archer (Sam Spade's sidekick) was shot. At the foot of the alley, the plaque reads in typical Hammett-ese: "On approximately this spot Miles Archer, partner of Sam Spade, was done in by Brigid O'Shaughnessy." A glance across Bush Street proves it's no mystery that this is Hammett territory; the perpendicular street is named Dashiell Hammett Street.

But apparently this was a popular spot for more than one literary legend. Directly across Bush Street from Burritt Alley, at 608 Bush, you'll find a plaque remembering Robert Louis Stevenson, who lodged here while living on 45¢ a day in 1879. He had come to San Francisco to be near Fanny Osbourne, who later would become his wife. The unknown, sick, and jobless writer was described by his landlady, Mrs. Carson, as "such a strange-looking shabby shock of a fellow."

Backtrack along Bush Street to Stockton Street, and continue on to 564 Bush St., where you'll find:

11. **Notre Dames-des-Victoires Church.** Built in 1913, this church's exterior is a replica of Notre Dame de Fourvière in Lyon, France. The present structure was built on the site of San Francisco's first French church, which was built in 1856 and, like just about everything else, destroyed in the 1906 quake. The less-destructive 1989 earthquake shook the church hard enough to force renovations, but today the building is a pristine place to worship and a good place to pop in if you're an admirer of stained glass.

Exit the church and continue along Bush Street to Grant Avenue. Cross Grant and Bush and you'll be in front of 352 Grant, the perfect spot to:

 Take a Break **Café de la Presse**'s dozens of foreign magazines, books, travel information, coffee drinks, and sidewalk eats reinforce the already prevalent notion that San Francisco is a very European city. Its prime location, directly across from the Chinatown gate, makes it one of the best spots to pull up a chair, get amped on java, snack on a pastry, and soak up the street-side scenics. If you're not ready to rest, hang tight because there's a great outdoor Italian cafe a few stops away.

When you depart from the cafe, turn left down Grant Avenue. At Post Street, cross Grant and make a left down Post. Toward the end of the block, enter no. 135, which is the famous storefront of:

12. **Gump's.** One of San Francisco's favorite house-and-home stores for more than 100 years, Gump's has a clientele that has sought out the finer things here since 1861. One glance around the refined and rather stuffy room and you know you're a long way from Pottery Barn. Here, gifts and treasures—especially contemporary ceramics and hand-blown glass, Asian antiques, jade and pearl jewelry, bath products, and table settings—are imported from all corners of the globe. Also noteworthy are the unique paper-weight collection and Gump's San Francisco Porcelains—beautifully detailed miniatures of San Francisco Victorians. Everything in the store is in its own way a work of art (a condition duly reflected in Gump's prices).

The department store also has its own art gallery, which displays contemporary works.

Exit Gump's and make a right. Make another right at Kearny Street, and on your right you'll soon run into the beginning of:

13. **Maiden Lane.** There's no trace of its previous life, but when this city was in its beginnings, Maiden Lane was anything but the type of street where designer boutiques such as Chanel would set up shop. It was previously known as Morton Alley, and a walk down here promised free glimpses of prostitutes who hung half-dressed from windows, tempting passersby with sexual services for a tri-fle. There might have been lots of lovin' going on, but the story goes that there was plenty of rage, too; murders in the alley alone averaged about one per week. The fire

The Gump Brothers

The Gump brothers, Solomon and Gustave, arrived in San Francisco from Germany in 1850 hoping, like everyone else who was heading west, to strike it rich. They opened a frame-and-mirror shop, which did well because there were many newly wealthy people in the city who were looking to decorate their homes. Later, Solomon began traveling the world looking for merchandise. Each time he returned, he brought back statuettes, paintings, sculptures, and porcelains for his own personal collection. His house became so full of these treasures that he was forced to take them to the shop and sell them. The Gumps' department store opened in 1861.

After 1900, Abraham Livingston Gump, who was nearly blind, took over the family business. It is he who is credited with having established Gump's as the leading dealer in Asian arts and antiquities on the West Coast.

following the 1906 earthquake burned the brothels to the ground, allowing the city's sleaziest strip to start anew. Apparently prostitution wasn't part of the plan, so the street name and reputation were changed to encourage a different sort of bartering. In recent years, high rents and dwindling foot traffic have made it difficult for stores to stay open on this upscale pedestrian street. But visitors seem to have no problem finding the Chanel boutique, and there's always a crowd at the umbrella-covered cafe tables where you can lunch while looking out onto Union Square.

After strolling the first block of the 2-block-long lane, make a right on Grant. Cross both Grant and Post to arrive at:

14. **Shreve & Co.,** 200 Post, a jeweler and the oldest retailer in the city, which was established in 1862 at another location but moved to this site just before the 1906 earthquake. Miraculously, it was one of the few buildings left

standing when the rubble and flames settled. Today Shreve & Co. still ornaments the well-to-do with gold, silver, and precious jewels.

Drop by to browse their new pieces or their vintage collection, but be warned: Once you get in the door it'll be hard not to find a trinket that you'll want to take home with you. On the bright side, even the biggest baubles won't weigh you down during your neighborhood tour.

Return to Maiden Lane and make a right onto the block you've yet to explore. On your right, at 140 Maiden Lane, is the home of the:

15. **Xanadu Gallery,** a gallery featuring folk art and antiquities from around the world. This building is the only one in the city designed by Frank Lloyd Wright (1949). It is said to be the precursor to the architect's design for the Guggenheim Museum in New York and features a similar spiral design, except on a smaller scale.

Continue west on Maiden Lane. Toward the end of the block, nearing Stockton Street, you'll see a group of umbrella-covered tables in the center of the road (it's open to foot traffic only). You might want to:

Take a Break **Mocca,** at 175 Maiden Lane, is one of the area's sexiest Italian delis. Inside you'll find simple sandwiches, cooked items like chicken, pasta or fruit salads, and pastries in a classically Italian atmosphere. If the weather's right, it's more fun to sit outside where you can people-watch over a mocha anytime from 10:30am to 5:30pm (they begin lunch service at 11am). FYI, bring cash because they don't accept credit cards.

When you're done, continue to the end of the block (Stockton) facing Union Square. Make a right here and cross both Post and Stockton streets. Just north of the corner, at 345 Stockton, enter the:

16. **Grand Hyatt.** Take the elevator to the 36th floor, where just to the right of the elevator, you'll find Club 36, which has the ambience of a hotel lobby but a view from the heavens. A wall of windows faces north, allowing you to survey Alcatraz, Coit Tower, and Fisherman's Wharf (fog permitting).

Walk out of the bar to your left to check out the eastern and southern views, where you'll see bits of the Bay Bridge and Berkeley peeking out from behind the Financial District's high-rises; the lush patch of green that makes up Yerba Buena Gardens; and standing solo, the towering, impossible-to-ignore Marriott Hotel. It was designed in 1989 by architect Anthony Lumsden and is both loved and loathed by San Franciscans. Some liken it to a mirrored jukebox—others to the world's largest parking meter. But for better or for worse, it is now a significant part of the downtown skyline. It's worth noting that this part of town, once characterized solely by warehouses and underground-style night clubs, is becoming more and more of an attraction thanks to recent-comers such as SBC Park (the waterfront stadium where the San Francisco Giants baseball team play) and the ongoing addition of luxury condo high rises and restaurants. Behind it lies the industrial and shipping area of China Basin. Even there you'll find growth.

Exit the hotel and turn right down Stockton. Cross O'Farrell and make a left. When you reach Grant, go right. At Market Street go left again, and at 744 Market you'll find the:

17. **Wells Fargo Bank,** noteworthy for its 1910 Beaux Arts design.

If you look directly ahead from the bank (looking up Market St.), you'll see the Phelan Building, a classic example of flatiron-style architecture, whereby a building is shaped to a triangular parcel of land. Here, you get a fantastic view of the structure, which stretches on for blocks and comes together in a point directly in front of you.

From the Wells Fargo Bank, turn back and follow Market Street to Hallidie Plaza at the corner of Powell and Market streets, where you'll find the San Francisco Convention & Visitors Bureau (down a flight of stairs). It offers a slew of tourist information. You can also catch BART or Muni trains here. Better yet, catch the Powell Street cable car and take a leisurely ride up Nob Hill and down to Fisherman's Wharf.

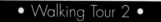

Chinatown: History, Culture, Dim Sum & Then Some

Start: Corner of Grant Avenue and Bush Street.

Public Transportation: Bus: 2, 3, 4, 9X, 15, 30, 38, 45, or 76.

Finish: Commercial Street between Montgomery and Kearny streets.

Time: 2 hours, not including museum or shopping stops.

Best Times: Daylight hours, when there's the most action.

Worst Times: Too early or too late, because shops are closed and no one is milling around.

Hills That Could Kill: None.

From the looks of things today, you'd never know what an important role the area now called Chinatown played in the development of the city. However, in essence, today's San Francisco was born and reared within these few square blocks.

In 1846, when the American flag was raised to declare American ownership of this region, it was done here at Portsmouth Square (then Portsmouth Plaza). In 1849, when gold-rush fever brought thousands of ships and fortune seekers from all around the world, they docked here along the shore, which was located (before the addition of landfill) at what is now Montgomery Street. This very area became the town's epicenter through the gold-rush years, and as a result the city's growth expanded from this neighborhood outward in all directions. And from the beginning, immigrants were here to witness the evolution and play a critical part in it.

When the first Chinese immigrants came to San Francisco around 1848, they found a very small town centered on Portsmouth Plaza. Like everyone else, they began settling around the town square, but it wasn't until the gold rush that the Chinese truly flocked to the United States. Fleeing famine and the Opium Wars, they had nothing to lose and everything to gain by coming to the "Golden Mountain" of California. By 1850 the Chinese community had grown to over 4,000. But as gold became less plentiful, fortune-seeking pioneers began to see the Chinese as competition, and harsh discrimination ensued.

Over the next 2 decades, as the Chinese population expanded and became known as a reliable workforce, they were subjected to more and more extreme prejudice, suffering acts of persecution, robbery, beatings, and murder. In 1874, a group of San Francisco residents passed a set of resolutions against the Chinese and sent a copy of the resolution to President Grant. In 1877, during one particularly violent public outbreak, Chinese were pelted with bricks and forced to watch as their properties and businesses were smashed. In fact, dissemination against the Chinese ultimately led to the passage of the Chinese Exclusion Act in 1882, which effectively stopped Chinese immigration; it is estimated the Chinese population of San Francisco at that time was approximately 50,000. It wasn't until 1943, as a result of China's alliance with the United States during World War II, that immigration from China became possible again.

Even during its many years of turmoil, San Francisco's Chinese community never left what is now called Chinatown. As the city grew and the wealthy moved toward the hill and south of Market Street, the Chinese unified, maintained their culture and tradition, and against all adversity, developed the strongest ethnic community in San Francisco. Their tiny quadrant, bounded loosely by Broadway and by Stockton, Kearny, and Bush streets, is said to harbor one of the largest Chinese populations outside Asia. Daily proof is the crowds of Chinese residents who flock to the herbal stores, vegetable markets, restaurants, and businesses. On this walk, you'll learn why Chinatown remains intriguing to all who wind through its narrow, crowded streets, and how its origins are responsible for the city as we know it.

• • • • • • • • • • • • • • • •

To begin the tour, make your way to the corner of Bush Street and Grant Avenue, four blocks from Union Square and all the downtown buses, where you can't miss the:

1. **Chinatown Gateway Arch.** The division between downtown and Chinatown is abrupt. One minute you're in cosmopolitan Union Square, and the next you're in an entirely different—and exotic—world. The instant transformation takes place here, at the gateway to Chinatown.

   Traditional Chinese villages have ceremonial gates like this one, which was donated by the Chinese Chamber of Commerce. A lot less formal than those in China, this gate was built more for the benefit of the tourist industry than anything else. Note the Fu Dogs—traditional guards of Chinese temples—on either side and the dragons on top.

   Once you cross the threshold, you'll be at the beginning of Chinatown's portion of:

2. **Grant Avenue.** This strip is a mecca for tourists who wander in and out of gift shops offering a variety of unnecessary junk interspersed with quality imports. You'll also find decent restaurants and grocery stores frequented by Chinese residents, ranging from children to the oldest living people you've ever seen. Mixed in are other San

Chinatown

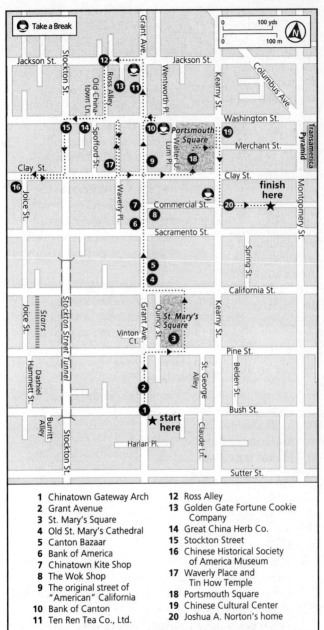

Francisco locals who come here for alternative medicines from the renowned herbal and acupuncture shops. Despite its commercialism, the street is crowded, colorful, and exotic enough to make you feel you're in the midst of something exciting.

Tear yourself away from the shops and turn right at the corner of Pine Street. Cross to the other side of Pine, and on your left you'll come to:

3. **St. Mary's Square,** where you'll find a huge metal-and-granite statue of Dr. Sun Yat-sen, the founder of the Republic of China. A native of Guangdong (Canton) Province, Sun Yat-sen led the rebellion that ended the reign of the Qing dynasty. He traveled all around the world in an effort to raise money for the revolution. While living in San Francisco, Sun founded a newspaper in the Montgomery Block.

The most notable feature about the statue, which was sculpted by Benjamino Bufano, is the figure's shining stainless-steel cloak. Sun Yat-sen, "Champion of Democracy" and "Proponent of Peace and Friendship among Nations," as the statue's pedestal proclaims, looks out over the benches and playground here and sometimes reflects a beautiful sunset in his "silver" cloak.

Note also the second monument in the square, which honors Chinese-American victims of both World Wars.

Walk to the other end of the square, toward California Street, turn left, cross California Street at Grant Street, and you'll be standing in front of:

4. **Old St. Mary's Cathedral.** The first Catholic cathedral in San Francisco and the site of the Chinese community's first English-language school, St. Mary's was built primarily by Chinese laborers and dedicated on Christmas Day 1854. Because it was built of brick (which was transported around Cape Horn) and granite (which came all the way from China), it was one of the lucky survivors of the 1906 earthquake, although its interior was gutted by the subsequent fire (and later renovated).

Step inside to find a written history of the church and turn-of-the-20th-century photos of San Francisco.

Upon leaving the church, take a right and walk to the corner of Grant Avenue and California Street, and then go right on Grant. Here you'll find a shop called the:

5. **Canton Bazaar,** at 616 Grant Ave. Of the barrage of knickknack and import shops lining Grant Avenue, this is one of the most popular, offering the gamut in Chinese wares and cheesy tourists' trinkets. Most noteworthy are the antique hand-carved furnishings and the Samurai sword collection. More affordable favorites include embroideries, porcelain, and a nifty selection of chopsticks.

Continue in the same direction on Grant Avenue, and cross Sacramento Street to the northwest corner of Sacramento and Grant. You'll be at the doorstep of the:

6. **Bank of America,** 701 Grant Ave, which is an example of traditional Chinese architectural style. Notice the dragons subtly portrayed on many parts of the building.

An interesting side note: Bank of America originally was created by A. P. Giannini, an Italian-American born in San Jose, California, who began the institution as the "Bank of Italy." He wanted to help immigrants who didn't have much money and couldn't get help from bigger banks.

Head in the same direction (north) on Grant, and a few doors down is the:

7. **Chinatown Kite Shop.** This store, located at 717 Grant Ave., has an assortment of flying objects, including attractive fish kites, nylon or cotton windsock kites, hand-painted Chinese paper kites, wood-and-paper biplanes, and pentagonal kites. The Chinese have a penchant for kites—particularly specially designed stunt kites, which they take up on the roofs of their houses and launch into kite fights with their neighbors. Kite fighting is taken very seriously as a sport, and as a result, the stakes can often be very high.

Although you won't see any kite fighting here, you might be able to find some flighty, easy-to-transport souvenirs.

Cross Grant, and you'll arrive at:

8. **The Wok Shop.** Here's where you can purchase just about any cleaver, wok, cookbook, or vessel you might need for Chinese-style cooking in your own kitchen. It's located at 718 Grant Ave.

   When you come out of The Wok Shop, go right. Walk past Commercial Street, and you'll arrive at the corner of Grant Avenue and Clay Street; cross Clay, and you'll be standing on the:

9. **Original Street of "American" California,** where an English seaman named William Richardson erected the first tent in 1835, making it the first place that an Anglo set up base in California.

   Continue north on Grant to Washington Street. Turn right, and at 743 Washington St. you will be standing in front of the:

10. **United Commercial Bank,** which boasts the oldest (from 1909) Asian-style edifice in Chinatown. The three-tiered temple-style building once housed the China Telephone Exchange, known as "China-5" until 1945. The exchange was famous for its operators who knew by heart the phone numbers of all of Chinatown's inhabitants—and also knew their habits so well that if a person was not at home, the operators often were able to track him or her down and send the call through.

    Before that, this building was the 1848 home of San Francisco's first newspaper, Sam Brannan's *California Star,* which helped spread the news that gold had been discovered in the hills of California.

    You're probably thirsty by now, so follow Washington Street a few doors down (east); on your right-hand side you can:

   Take a Break **Washington Bakery & Restaurant** (733 Washington St). No need to have a full meal here—the service can be abrupt. Do stop in, however, for a little potable adventure: snow red beans with ice cream. The sugary-sweet drink mixed with whole beans and ice cream is not something you're likely to have tried elsewhere, and it happens to be quite tasty. Whatever you do, don't fill up—a few blocks away, some wonderfully fresh dim sum awaits you. (*Note:* If the place is packed, either order a snack along with your drink or ask for takeout; the waitstaff is bound to be annoyed that you're holding up a table for a mere beverage.)

Head back to Grant Avenue, cross Washington Street, cross Grant, and follow the west side of Grant 1 block to no. 949, the location of:

11. **Ten Ren Tea Co., Ltd.** In this amazing shop you can sample a freshly brewed tea variety and check out the dozens of drawers and canisters labeled with more than 40 kinds of tea. Like Washington Bakery, Ten Ren offers unusual drinks worth trying: delightful hot or iced milk teas containing giant blobs of jelly or tapioca. Try black tea or green tea and enjoy the outstanding flavors and the giant balls of tapioca slipping around in your mouth.

Leave Ten Ren, make a left, and when you reach Jackson Street, make another left. On the left side, at 735 Jackson St., through the storefront window, you'll notice stacks of steaming wooden baskets and a Chinese cook. You've reached your snacking destination.

Take a Break It's the **House of Dim Sum**— nothing fancy, to be sure, but the dumplings are fresh, cheap, and delicious. Owners Cindy and Ben Yee are friendly, which is a plus in this sometimes abrupt community. Order at the counter: chive and shrimp dumplings; shark-fin dumplings; sweet buns; turnip cake; or sweet rice with chicken wrapped in a lotus leaf. Unless the three tables downstairs and more upstairs are taken, it's best to sit at one to enjoy your feast. (Last time I ate here it cost $7.60 for two people, drinks included!)

As you leave the House of Dim Sum, turn left so you're heading west on Jackson, and promptly make a left onto:

12. **Ross Alley.** As you walk along this narrow street, just one of the many alleyways that crisscrossed Chinatown to

accommodate the many immigrants who jammed into the neighborhood, it's not difficult to believe that this block once was rife with gambling dens.

As you follow the alley south, on the left side of the street you'll encounter the:

13. **Golden Gate Fortune Cookie Company,** at 56 Ross Alley. This store is little more than a tiny place where three women sit at a conveyer belt, folding messages into warm cookies as the manager invariably calls out to tourists, beckoning them to buy a big bag of the fortune-telling treats.

    You can purchase regular fortunes, unfolded flat cookies without fortunes, or, if you bring your own fortunes, custom cookies (I often do this when I'm having dinner parties) at around $6 for 50 cookies—a very cheap way to impress your friends! Or, of course, you can just take a peek and move on.

    As you exit the alley, cross Washington Street, take a right heading west on Washington, and you're in front of:

14. **Great China Herb Co.** For centuries, the Chinese have come to shops like this one, at 857 Washington St., which are full of exotic herbs, roots, and other natural substances. They buy what they believe will cure all types of ailments and ensure good health and long life. Thankfully, unlike owners in many similar area shops, Mr. and Mrs. Ho speak English, so you will not be met with a blank stare when you inquire what exactly is in each box, bag, or jar arranged along dozens of shelves. It is important to note that you should not use Chinese herbs without the guidance of a knowledgeable source such as an herb doctor. They may be natural, but they also can be quite powerful and are potentially harmful if misused.

    Take a left upon leaving the store and walk to:

15. **Stockton Street.** The section of Stockton Street between Broadway and Sacramento Street is where most of the residents of Chinatown do their daily shopping.

    One noteworthy part of this area's history is **Cameron House** (actually up the hill at 920 Sacramento St., near

Stockton St.), which was named after Donaldina Cameron (1869–1968). Called Lo Mo, or "the Mother," by the Chinese, she spent her life trying to free Chinese women who came to America in hopes of marrying well but who found themselves forced into prostitution and slavery. Today, the house still helps women free themselves from domestic violence.

A good stop if you're in the market for some jewelry is **Jade Galore** (1000 Stockton St. at Washington St.). Though the employees aren't exactly warm and fuzzy, they've got the goods. In addition to purveying jade jewelry, the store does a fair trade in diamonds.

After browsing at Jade Galore, you might want to wander up Stockton Street to absorb the atmosphere and street life of this less-tourist-oriented Chinese community before doubling back to Washington Street. At 1068 Stockton St. you'll find **AA Bakery & Café,** an extremely colorful bakery with Golden Gate Bridge–shaped cakes, bright green and pink snacks, moon cakes, and a flow of Chinese diners catching up over pastries. Another fun place at which to peek is **Gourmet Delight B.B.Q.,** at 1045 Stockton St., where barbecued duck and pork are supplemented by steamed pigs' feet and chicken feet. Everything's to go here, so if you grab a snack, don't forget napkins. Head farther north along the street and you'll see live fish and fowl awaiting their fate as the day's dinner.

Meander south on Stockton Street to Clay Street and turn west (right) onto Clay. Continue to 965 Clay St., location of the:

16. **Chinese Historical Society of America Museum.**
Founded in 1963, this museum (© 415/391-1188) has a small but fascinating collection that illuminates the role of Chinese immigrants in American history, particularly in San Francisco and the rest of California.

The interesting artifacts on display include a shrimp-cleaning machine; 19th-century clothing and slippers of the Chinese pioneers; Chinese herbs and scales; historic hand-carved and painted shop signs; and a series of photographs that document the development of Chinese culture in America.

The goal of this organization is not only to "study, record, acquire, and preserve all suitable artifacts and such cultural items as manuscripts, books, and works of art . . . which have a bearing on the history of the Chinese living in the United States of America," but also to "promote the contributions that Chinese Americans living in this country have made to the United States of America." It's an admirable and much-needed effort, considering what little recognition and appreciation the Chinese have received throughout American history.

The museum is open Tuesday through Friday from noon to 5pm and Saturday and Sunday from noon to 4pm. Admission is $3 adults, $2 for college students with ID and seniors, and $1 for kids 6 to 17.

Retrace your steps, heading east on Clay Street back toward Grant Avenue. Turn left onto:

17. **Waverly Place.** Also known as "The Street of Painted Balconies," Waverly Place is probably Chinatown's most popular side street or alleyway because of its painted balconies and colorful architectural details—a sort of Chinese-style New Orleans street. You can admire the architecture only from the ground, because most of the buildings are private family associations or temples.

One temple you can visit (but make sure it's open before you climb the long, narrow stairway) is the **Tin How Temple,** at 125 Waverly Place. Accessible via the stairway three floors up, this incense-laden sanctuary, decorated in traditional black, red, and gold lacquered wood, is a house of worship for Chinese Buddhists, who come here to pray, meditate, and send offerings to their ancestors and to Tin How, the Queen of the Heavens and Goddess of the Seven Seas. There are no scheduled services, but you are welcome to visit. Just remember to quietly respect those who are here to pray, and try to be as unobtrusive as possible. It is customary to give a donation or buy a bundle of incense during your visit.

Once you've finished exploring Waverly Place, walk east on Clay Street, past Grant Avenue, and continue until you come upon the block-wide urban playground that is also the most important site in San Francisco's history:

18. **Portsmouth Square.** This very spot was the center of the region's first township, which was called Yerba Buena before it was renamed San Francisco in 1847. Around 1846, before any semblance of a city had taken shape, this plaza lay at the foot of the bay's eastern shoreline. There were fewer than 50 non–Native American residents in the settlement, there were no substantial buildings to speak of, and the few boats that pulled into the cove did so less than a block from where you're sitting.

    But the following years brought devastating change. In 1846, when California was claimed as a U.S. territory, the marines who landed here named the square after their ship, the USS *Portsmouth.* (Today, a bronze plaque marks the spot where they raised the U.S. flag.)

    Yerba Buena remained a modest township until the gold rush of 1849 when, over the next 2 years, the population grew from under 1,000 to over 19,000, as gold seekers from around the world made their way here.

    When the square became too crowded, long wharves were constructed to support new buildings above the bay. Eventually, the entire area became landfill. That was almost 150 years ago, but today the square still serves as an important meeting place for neighborhood Chinese— a sort of communal outdoor living room.

    Throughout the day, the square is heavily trafficked by children and—in large part—by elderly men, who gamble over Chinese cards. If you arrive early in the morning, you might come across people practicing tai chi.

    It is said that Robert Louis Stevenson used to love to sit on a bench here and watch life go by. (At the northeast corner of the square, you'll find a monument to his memory, consisting of a model of the *Hispañola,* the ship in Stevenson's novel *Treasure Island,* and an excerpt from his "Christmas Sermon.")

    Once you've had your fill of the square, exit to the east, at Kearny Street. Directly across the street, at 750 Kearny, is the Holiday Inn. Cross the street, enter the hotel, and take the elevator to the third floor, where you'll find the:

19. **Chinese Culture Center.** This center is oriented toward both the community and tourists, offering interesting

display cases of Chinese art, and a gallery with rotating exhibits of Asian art and writings. The center is open Tuesday through Saturday from 10am to 4pm.

When you leave the Holiday Inn, take a left on Kearny and go 3 short blocks to Commercial Street. Take a left onto Commercial and note that you are standing on the street once known as the site of:

20. **Joshua A. Norton's Home.** Norton, the self-proclaimed "Emperor of the United States and Protector of Mexico," used to walk around the streets in an old brass-buttoned military uniform, sporting a hat with a "dusty plume." He lived in a fantasy world, and San Franciscans humored him at every turn.

Norton was born around 1815 in the British Isles and sailed as a young man to South Africa, where he served as a colonial rifleman. He came to San Francisco in 1849 with $40,000 and proceeded to double and triple his fortune in real estate. Unfortunately for him, he next chose to go into the rice business. While Norton was busy cornering the market and forcing prices up, several ships loaded with rice arrived unexpectedly in San Francisco's harbor. The rice market was suddenly flooded, and Norton was forced into bankruptcy. He left San Francisco for about 3 years and must have experienced a breakdown (or revelation) of some sort, for upon his return, Norton thought he was an emperor.

Instead of ostracizing him, however, San Franciscans embraced him as their own homegrown lunatic and gave him free meals. Gertrude Atherton said that "he walked majestically into banks, stores, and mercantile houses and presented formal bills for their taxes. The sums were small and were paid with good-natured humor. They were acknowledged by a formal receipt, decorated with a great seal, and inscribed, 'Norton I, Emperor of the U.S.A.' The City Council voted him one of the expenses of the city treasury."

When Emperor Norton died in 1880 (while sleeping at the corner of California St. and Grant Ave.) approximately 10,000 people passed by his coffin, which was bought with money raised at the Pacific Union Club, and more than 30,000 people participated in the funeral procession. Today you won't see a trace of his character, but it's fun to imagine him cruising the street.

From here, if you've still got an appetite, you should go directly to 631 Kearny (at Clay St.), home of:

Take a Break **The R&G Lounge** is a sure thing for tasty $5 rice-plate specials, chicken with black-bean sauce, and gorgeously tender and tangy R&G Special Beef.

Otherwise, you might want to backtrack on Commercial Street to Grant Avenue, take a left, and follow Grant back to Bush Street, the entrance to Chinatown. You'll be at the beginning of the Union Square area, where you can catch any number of buses (especially on Market St.) or cable cars or do a little shopping. Or you might backtrack to Grant, take a right (north), and follow Grant to the end. You'll be at Broadway and Columbus, the beginning of North Beach, where you can venture onward for our North Beach tour (see Walking Tour 3).

Getting to Know North Beach

Start: Intersection of Montgomery Street, Columbus Avenue, and Washington Street.

Public Transportation: Bus: 10, 12, 15, 30X, or 41.

Finish: Washington Square.

Time: 3 hours, including a stop for lunch.

Best Times: Monday through Saturday between 11am and 4pm.

Worst Times: Sunday, when shops are closed.

Hills That Could Kill: The Montgomery Street hill from Broadway to Vallejo Street; otherwise, this is an easy walk.

Along with Chinatown, North Beach is one of the city's oldest neighborhoods. Originally the Latin Quarter, it became the city's Italian district when Italian immigrants moved "uphill" in the early 1870s, crossing Broadway from the Jackson Square area and settling in. They quickly established restaurants, cafes, bakeries, and other businesses familiar to them from their homeland. The "Beat Generation" helped put North Beach on the map, with the likes of Jack Kerouac and Allen Ginsberg holding court in the area's cafes during the 1950s. Although most of the original Beat poets are gone, their spirit lives on in North Beach, which is still a haven for bohemian artists and writers. The neighborhood, thankfully, retains its Italian village feel; it's a place where residents from all walks of life enjoy taking time for conversation over pastries and frothy cappuccinos.

Named after a beach that once extended from Telegraph Hill to Russian Hill but has long since been replaced by a land-fill, North Beach remains the Italian center of San Francisco. You can get Italian food on practically every block (I'll point out plenty of spots for a quick snack and caffeine fix), and chances are you'll see small groups of older Italian expatriates chatting on a bench or playing bocce in the park. You might even witness an Italian wedding at Saints Peter and Paul Church.

This tour will take you from Washington Street up through North Beach. In general, you'll be following Columbus Avenue and taking some detours to one side or the other. You will visit a small corner of San Francisco's original Financial District, including historic Jackson Square, before proceeding to many of the beatniks' favorite hangouts, including the City Lights Bookstore. Finally, you'll end up in Washington Square. Along the way you'll pass by some great shopping and music venues, which I'll point out throughout the tour. Be sure to schedule your tour to include a leisurely lunch or dinner at one of the sidewalk cafes, easily my pick for the top North Beach pastime.

• • • • • • • • • • • • • • • •

If there's one landmark you can't miss, it's the familiar building on the corner of Montgomery Street and Columbus Avenue, the:

1. **TransAmerica Pyramid.** Noted for its spire (which rises 212 ft. above the top floor) and its "wings" (which

begin at the 29th floor and stop at the spire), this pyramid is San Francisco's tallest building and a hallmark of the skyline. You might want to take a peek at one of the rotating art exhibits in the lobby or go around to the right and into ½-acre Redwood Park, which is part of the TransAmerica Center. Year-round you can sit here and enjoy the greenery, redwood trees, and the fountain.

The TransAmerica Pyramid occupies part of the 600 block of Montgomery Street, which once held a historic building called:

2. **The Montgomery Block,** originally four stories high, making it the tallest building in the West when it was built in 1853. San Franciscans called it "Halleck's Folly" because it was built on a raft of redwood logs that had been bolted together and floated at the edge of the ocean (which was right at Montgomery St. at that time). This construction proved to be a bit of architectural genius by Captain Henry Wager Halleck that, in fact, helped the building withstand several earthquakes, including the earthquake of 1906.

The building was demolished in 1959 but is fondly remembered for its historic importance as the power center of the city. Its tenants included artists and writers of all kinds, among them Jack London, Ambrose Bierce, Bret Harte, and Mark Twain. These men would gather nearly every day at the marble-floored, mahogany Bank Exchange bar where beer was drawn from Wedgwood taps. The proprietor of the bar, a Scotsman named Duncan Nicol, invented the bar's famous drink, Pisco Punch (with a Peruvian brandy base)—it was so strong that patrons were allowed only two glasses at a sitting. These literati also liked to hang out at Coppa's, which opened later and was located on the Merchant Street corner of the Montgomery Block. Coppa's is where bohemian San Francisco was born.

Everybody who was anybody hung out here in the palm-dotted lobby. It was described by Idwal Jones, a Montgomery Block scholar, as the "social vortex of the city, of all of California" and the "meeting place of all professions." Everything, including banks, theaters, shops,

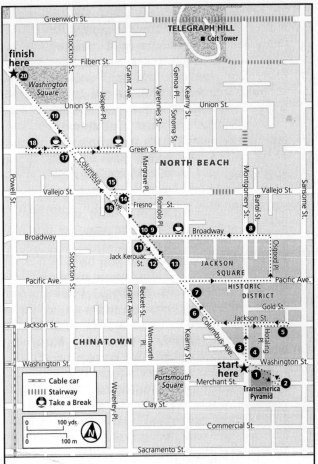

1 Transamerica Pyramid
2 The Montgomery Block
3 Original Transamerica Building
4 Golden Era Building
5 400 block of Jackson Square
6 Columbus Tower
7 140 Columbus Avenue
8 1010 Montgomery Street
9 hungry i
10 Former site of the Condor Club
11 City Lights Bookstore

12 Vesuvio
13 Specs' Adler Museum Café and Tosca Café
14 Caffè Trieste
15 Biordi Art Imports
16 Molinari Delicatessen
17 North Beach Museum
18 Club Fugazi
19 Mario's Bohemian Cigar Store
20 Washington Square

and newspaper offices (if they weren't here), was within walking distance from the Montgomery Block. The offices were occupied by lawyers and judges; the shops were leased to custom tailors, milliners, jewelers, and print sellers. Agoston Haraszthy, the founder of the California wine industry, leased space in the basement; and gold was refined, cast into ingots, and lowered into the vaults at Adams and Co. on the Merchant Street side. Sun Yat-sen's newspaper offices were here (see Walking Tour 2, stop 3 for more info on Sun Yat-sen), as was bohemian poet George Sterling's fourth-floor office, where he would work on his verse in his robe each morning (and in which he hung approximately 20 portraits of himself).

From the southeast corner of Montgomery and Washington streets, look across Washington to the corner of Columbus Avenue, and you'll see the:

3. **Original TransAmerica Building,** a Beaux Arts flat-iron-shaped building covered in terra cotta, located at 4 Columbus Ave. Built for the Banco Populare Italiano Operaia Fugazi in 1909; it was originally a two-story building to which a third floor was added in 1916. In 1928, Fugazi merged his bank with the Bank of America, which was started by A. P. Giannini (see Walking Tour 2, stop 6, for details on this bank), who also created the TransAmerica Corporation, a holding company he head-quartered here until 1972, when it moved into the Transamerica Pyramid across the street. The building now houses a Church of Scientology.

Cross Washington Street and continue north on Montgomery Street to no. 730, the:

4. **Golden Era Building,** erected around 1852 and named after the literary magazine, *Golden Era,* which was published here. Some of the young writers who worked on the magazine were known as "The Bohemians"; they included Samuel Clemens (aka Mark Twain) and Bret Harte (who began as a typesetter here). Clemens and Harte were different in every way possible—Clemens was a sloppy dresser but a quick-witted writer; Harte was

something of a dandy, but suffered over every word he put on paper—yet they became the best of friends.

Backtrack a few dozen feet and stop for a minute to admire the exterior of the annex, at no. 722 (marked by a faded black-and-white striped awning but currently under renovation). The **Belli Annex,** as it is currently known, is registered as a historic landmark. Built between 1853 and 1854 on the foundations of an 1849 building, the three-story Italianate brick structure was the original home of Freemasonry in California. A plaque tells us that it was here on October 17, 1949, that Lodge number 1 had its first meeting.

Continue north on Washington Street, and take the first right onto Jackson Street. Continue until you hit the:

5. **400 Block of Jackson Square,** where you'll find some of the only commercial buildings to survive the 1906 earthquake and fire. The building at no. 415 Jackson (ca. 1853) served as headquarters for the Ghirardelli Chocolate Company from 1855 to 1894. The Hotaling Building (no. 451) was built in 1866 and features pediments and quoins of cast iron applied over the brick walls. At no. 441 is another of the buildings that survived the disaster of 1906. Constructed between 1850 and 1852 with ship masts for interior supporting columns, it served as the French Consulate from 1865 to 1876.

You've probably already noticed that this is one of San Francisco's antiques centers, but equally important, it is the architectural center. In addition to some of the most prestigious antiques dealerships in town, you'll find several different architectural supply shops and design firms. One of the greatest architecture bookstores around is **William Stout Architecture Books,** at 804 Montgomery St. (on the corner of Jackson and Montgomery sts.). If you happen to be looking for something that's a little esoteric, it's very likely they'll have it here. This incredible store evolved from a personal collection of only a few dozen books in William Stout's apartment to the current stock of (approximately) 11,000 hard-to-find books and magazines. William Stout is open

Monday through Friday from 10am to 6:30pm and Saturday from 10am to 5:30pm.

Cross the street, and backtrack on Jackson Street. Continue toward the intersection of Columbus Avenue and Jackson Street. Turn right on Columbus and look across the street for the small triangular building at the junction of Kearny Street and Columbus Avenue:

6. **Columbus Tower,** also known as the Sentinel Building. If you walk a little farther, and then turn around and look back down Columbus, you'll be able to get a better look at Columbus Tower. The flat-iron beauty, a building shaped to a triangular site, went up between 1905 and 1907. Movie director and producer Francis Ford Coppola bought and restored it in the mid-1970s; it is now home to his film production company, American Zoetrope Studios. The building's cafe showcases all things Niebaum-Coppola (as in Coppola's winery)—including olive oil, Parmesan cheese, and wine. It's a great place to stop for a glass of wine, an espresso, or a thin-crusted pizza snack. This is one of the few pre-1906 earthquake buildings left in the city center.

Across the street from Columbus Tower on Columbus Avenue is:

7. **140 Columbus Ave.** Once home to the performance venue known as the Purple Onion, this place has seen many famous headliners, often before they were famous. Phyllis Diller, who's now so big that she's famous for something as simple as her laugh, was still struggling when she played a 2-week engagement here in the late 1950s. Alex Haley tried to interview her during that engagement, and she told him, "No, not yet, baby. I'm not big enough for you to be able to sell it, and you're not big enough to get it sold in the right place." Six years later, while working as a reporter for the *Saturday Evening Post,* Haley saw that Diller was playing at the **hungry i** (see stop 9, below), so he went in and knocked on her dressing-room door. She jumped out of her chair and hugged him, saying, "Baby, we've made it." (She also was one of the first people to contact Haley after his success with

Roots.) Among many other performers, one who stood out was Maya Angelou, author of *I Know Why the Caged Bird Sings* and the poet who read at the inauguration of President Clinton; she sang here during the 1950s.

Continue north on Columbus, and then turn right on Pacific Avenue. After you cross Montgomery Street, you'll find brick-lined **Osgood Place** on the left. A registered historic landmark, it is one of the few quiet—and car-free—little alleyways left in the city. Stroll up Osgood and go left on Broadway to:

8. **1010 Montgomery St.** This is where Allen Ginsberg lived when he wrote his legendary poem "Howl," first performed on October 13, 1955, in a converted auto-repair shop at the corner of Fillmore and Union streets (in a different part of town). By the time Ginsberg finished reading, he was crying and the audience was going wild. Jack Kerouac proclaimed, "Ginsberg, this poem will make you famous in San Francisco." Poet Kenneth Rexroth was more visionary when he said it would make him famous not only in San Francisco but "from bridge to bridge." The reading that night did more than make Ginsberg famous: it also catapulted his fellow Beat poets into the limelight.

Continue along Broadway toward Columbus Avenue. This stretch of Broadway is San Francisco's answer to New York's Times Square, complete with strip clubs and peep shows that are being pushed aside by restaurants, clubs, and an endless crowd of visitors. It's among the most sought-after locations in the city as more and more profitable restaurants and clubs spring up. Keep walking west on Broadway, and on the right side of the street, you'll come to **Black Oak Books,** 540 Broadway. It sells new and used discount books and is worth a quick trip inside for a good, cheap read.

A few dozen yards farther up Broadway is the current location of the:

9. **hungry i.** Now a seedy strip club (at 546 Broadway), the original hungry i (at 599 Jackson St., which is under construction for senior housing) was owned and operated by

the vociferous "Big Daddy" Nordstrom. He and his friend Mark Adams gave the club its name one day as they were driving around the city. Adams suggested the name "Hungry Id," for "the inner man's search." Big Daddy didn't like that name too much, so Adams shortened it to "hungry i," with lowercase letters, and Big Daddy roared, "Hey, what a helluva name for the club."

Not too long after he named the club, he traded it for a restaurant (losing money at the time) that was owned by Enrico Banducci. Banducci was a wildly generous man who demonstratively loved his friends—his restaurant was failing because he was giving away too much food. He took on the hungry i, which wasn't worth much at that time, and turned it into a roaring success.

In keeping with the idea of the "inner man's search," Enrico thought that there should be "no big frills at the club, so the visitor could feel that "right now, you're what counts. Not how it looks, or any diamonds you're wearing. but [it's] the inner man that counts." If you had been here while Enrico Banducci was in charge, you would have found only a plain room with an exposed brick wall and director's chairs around small tables.

A who's who of nightclub entertainers fortified their careers at the original hungry i, including Lenny Bruce, Billie Holiday (who first sang "Strange Fruit" there), Bill Cosby, Richard Pryor, Woody Allen, and Barbra Streisand.

At the corner of Broadway and Columbus Avenue, at 300 Columbus Ave., you will see the:

10. **Former Site of the Condor Club,** where Carol Doda scandalously bared her breasts and danced topless for the first time in 1964. Note the bronze plaque claiming the Condor Club as BIRTHPLACE OF THE WORLD'S FIRST TOPLESS & BOTTOMLESS ENTERTAINMENT. Go inside what is now the Condor Sports Bar and have a look at the framed newspaper clippings that hang around the dining room. From the elevated back room, you can see Doda's old dressing room and, on the floor below, an outline of the piano that would descend from the second floor with her

atop it—later becoming infamous for crushing a doorman to his death as he made whoopee with a dancer.

The Condor Club credited itself with having started the strip joint craze that took off after completely nude dancers were seen here. The section of Broadway that was home to these "joints" became known as "The Strip." San Francisco's moral minority, however, was a minor round in 1991 when the Condor Club's Carol Doda sign—a well-proportioned rendering of the city's celebrated stripper—was torn down and the topless bar was converted into a bistro.

When you leave the Condor Sports Bar, cross to the south side of Broadway. Note the mural of jazz musicians painted on the entire side of the building directly across Columbus Avenue. Diagonally across the intersection from the Condor Sports Bar is the:

11. **City Lights Booksellers & Publishers.** Founded in 1953 and owned by one of the first Beat poets to arrive in San Francisco, Lawrence Ferlinghetti, City Lights is now a city landmark and literary mecca. Located at 261 Columbus Ave., it's one of the last of the Beat-era hangouts in operation. At the time Ferlinghetti started the store, most people thought paperback books were inferior to hardcovers in both the quality of the paper and the quality of the content, but Ferlinghetti forced people to think differently about them. He made great literature available by stocking his bookstore with less costly editions.

An active participant in the Beat movement, Ferlinghetti established his shop as a meeting place where writers and bibliophiles could (and still do) attend poetry readings and other events. A vibrant part of the literary scene, the well-stocked bookshop prides itself on its collection of art, poetry, and political paperbacks.

Ferlinghetti has always been a maverick bookseller and publisher. He was the first to publish and sell Allen Ginsberg's controversial poem "Howl," and his arrest in 1957 for selling obscene materials brought the bookstore to the attention of the nation. Ferlinghetti was acquitted when the judge ruled that "Howl" had "redeeming social value"—a decision that paved the way for publication of the like of D. H. Lawrence's *Lady Chatterly's Lover.* City Lights Press continues to publish about a dozen avant-garde works every year.

Upon exiting City Lights bookstore, turn right, cross aptly named Jack Kerouac Street, and stop at the bar on your right:

12. **Vesuvio,** which became a favorite hangout of the Beats. The bar once advertised the sale of the Beatnik Kit; in the front window was displayed a mannequin wearing a black sweater, sunglasses, a mustache, and a pair of sandals. Even today, Vesuvio, which opened in 1949, maintains its original bohemian atmosphere. The bar is located at 255 Columbus Ave. (at Jack Kerouac St.) and dates from 1913. It is an excellent example of pressed-tin architecture.

You'll probably still see a couple of regulars hanging out in the front window playing cards or chess or reading the newspaper. The gas-fired chandelier hanging over the bar, nearly 100 years old, is a beauty, and the walls are hung with old black-and-whites of many of the Beat poets, as well as the art of local artists. A sign over the bar explains that no food is served on the premises, but visitors are welcome to bring their lunch and have a drink. Also over the bar is a ribald quotation: "T'was a woman that drove me to drink and I never had the decency to thank her." You can even order drinks named after the Beats, like the "Jack Kerouac."

Facing Vesuvio across Columbus Avenue is another favorite spot of the Beat Generation:

13. **Spec's Adler Museum Café.** Located at 12 Saroyan Place, this is one of the city's funkiest bars, a small, dimly lit watering hole with ceiling-hung maritime flags and exposed brick walls crammed with memorabilia. Within the bar is a minimuseum that consists of a few glass cases filled with mementos brought by seamen who frequented the pub from the '40s and onward.

From here, walk back up Columbus across Broadway to Grant Avenue. Turn right on Grant, and continue until you come to Vallejo Street. At 601 Vallejo St. (at Grant Ave.) is:

14. **Caffè Trieste.** Yet another favorite spot of the Beats and founded by Gianni Giotta in 1956, Caffè Trieste is still run by family members. The quintessential San Francisco coffeehouse, Trieste features opera on the jukebox, and the real thing, performed by the Giottas, on Saturday afternoons. Any day of the week is a good one to stop in for a cappuccino or espresso—the beans are roasted right next door.

Go left out of Caffè Trieste onto Vallejo Street, turn right on Columbus Avenue, and bump into the loveliest shop in all of North Beach, located at 412 Columbus Ave.:

15. **Biordi Art Imports,** which has carried imported hand-painted majolica pottery from the hill towns of central Italy for more than 50 years. Some of the colorful patterns date from the 14th century. Biordi handpicks its artisans, and its catalog includes biographies of those who are currently represented.

Across Columbus Avenue, at the corner of Vallejo Street, is the:

16. **Molinari Delicatessen.** This deli, located at 373 Columbus Ave., has been selling its pungent, air-dried salamis since 1896. Ravioli and tortellini are made in the back of the shop, but it's the mouthwatering selection of cold salads, cheeses, and marinades up front that captures the attention of most folks. Each Italian sub is big enough for two hearty appetites.

Walk north to the lively intersection of Columbus, Green, and Stockton, and look for the U.S. Bank at 1435 Stockton St. On the second floor of the bank, you'll find the:

17. **North Beach Museum,** displaying historical artifacts that tell the story of North Beach, Chinatown, and Fisherman's Wharf. Just before you enter the museum, you'll find a framed, handwritten poem by Beat poet Lawrence Ferlinghetti that captures his impressions of this

primarily Italian neighborhood. After you pass through the glass doors, you'll see many photographs of some of the first Chinese and Italian immigrants, as well as pictures of San Francisco after the 1906 earthquake. You can visit the museum any time the bank is open (unfortunately, it's closed on weekends), and admission is free.

Now backtrack toward Columbus Avenue and go left on Green Street to 678 Green St., location of:

18. **Club Fugazi.** It doesn't look like much from the outside, but Fugazi Hall was donated to the city (and more important, the North Beach area) by John Fugazi, the founder of the Italian bank that was taken over by A. P. Giannini and turned into the original TransAmerica Corporation.

For many years, Fugazi Hall has been staging the zany and whimsical musical revue *Beach Blanket Babylon.* The show evolved from Steve Silver's Rent-a-Freak service, which consisted of a group of partygoers who would attend parties dressed as any number of characters in outrageous costumes. The fun caught on and soon became *Beach Blanket Babylon.*

If you love comedy, you'll love this show. We don't want to spoil it for you by telling you what it's about, but if you get tickets and they're in an unreserved-seat section, you should arrive fairly early because you'll be seated around small cocktail tables on a first-come, first-served basis. (Two sections have reserved seating, four don't, and all of them frequently sell out weeks in advance; however, sometimes it is possible to get tickets at the last minute on weekdays.) You'll want to be as close to the stage as possible. This supercharged show is definitely worth the price of admission. Call © **415/421-4222** or go to their website at www.beachblanketbabylon.com.

Head back the way you came on Green Street, and before you get to Columbus Avenue, be sure to stop in at:

Take a Break O'Reilly's Irish Pub (622 Green St.) is a homey watering hole that dishes out good, hearty Irish food and a fine selection of beers (including Guinness, of course) that are best enjoyed at one of the sidewalk tables. Always a conversation piece is the mural of Irish authors peering from the back wall. (How many can you name?)

As you come out of O'Reilly's, turn left, cross Columbus Avenue, and then take a left on Columbus. Proceed 1 block northwest to:

19. **Mario's Bohemian Cigar Store.** Located at 566 Columbus Ave., across the street from Washington Square, this is one of North Beach's most popular neighborhood hangouts. No, it doesn't sell cigars, but the cramped and casual space overlooking Washington Square does sell killer focaccia sandwiches and coffee drinks. The historic, tiny, and charmingly threadbare bar has long been a popular meeting place for aged Sicilians and Beat poets, though nowadays it attracts all types, including the occasional tourist in search of a cigar.

Our next stop, directly across Union Street, is:

20. **Washington Square,** one of the oldest parks in the city. The land was designated a public park in 1847 and has undergone many changes since then. Its current landscaping dates from 1955. Even though it's called a "square," this little oasis in the middle of such a bustling neighborhood sort of lost its square status when Columbus Avenue was laid out and one of its four corners was lopped off. Why isn't it named Columbus Square? Because the park was named in the 1850s, before Montgomery Avenue was changed to Columbus Avenue.

You'll notice **Saints Peter and Paul Church** (the religious center for the neighborhood's Italian community) on the northwest end. Designed in 1922, the cathedral took 20 years to build. Known as "the Church of the Fisherman" (because it was the primary church for the Italian fishermen who lived here), it is the point of origin for processions that honor the blessing of the fishing fleet every October. Take a few moments to go inside and check out the traditional Italian interior. Note that this is the church in which baseball great Joe DiMaggio married his first wife, Dorothy Arnold. He wasn't allowed to marry Marilyn Monroe here because he had been divorced. He married Monroe at City Hall and came here for publicity photos.

On the Columbus Avenue side of the park, you'll find a bronze statue of three firemen and a damsel in distress, erected in 1933 to honor San Francisco's fireman at the bequest of Lillie Hitchcock Coit (see Walking Tour 4, stop 4, for more information). The statue was supposed to be erected in front of Coit Tower (which, ironically, is fronted by a statue of Christopher Columbus), but somehow ended up in Washington Square.

A statue of Benjamin Franklin, donated by H. D. Cogswell (a wealthy, eccentric dentist and prohibitionist) in 1879, stands over a time capsule at the center of the park. Emptied in 1979, the capsule previously held a number of Victorian tracts. Currently the capsule is home to a pair of Levi's jeans, a bottle of wine, a Ferlinghetti poem, and a Hoodoo Rhythm Devils album. Chances are that you won't be around for the next opening—it's in 2079. Cogwell, an ardent teetotaler, wanted the citizens of San Francisco to drink more water than wine, hence the indentations at the base of the statue where water once flowed.

At the other side of the park, on the Stockton Street side, is a bench with a plaque in dedication of Irving Stone, Jack London's biographer, who was born near here in 1903.

Today the park is a pleasant place in which to soak up the sun, read a book, or chat with a retired Italian octogenarian who has seen the city grow and change.

From here, you can see the famous **Coit Tower** at the top of Telegraph Hill to the northwest (see Walking Tour 4, stop 4, for details). If you'd like to get back to your starting point at Columbus and Montgomery streets, walk south (away from the water) on Columbus.

The Storied
Steps of
Telegraph Hill

Start: Washington Square.

Public Transportation: Bus: 15, 30, 39, 41, or 45; cable car: Powell-Mason.

Finish: Levi Strauss Plaza.

Time: 2 to 3 hours, not including shopping time.

Best Times: Between 10am and 5pm, so you'll get a chance to go into Coit Tower, open from 10am to 6pm daily.

Worst Times: Before 9am and after 5pm.

Hills That Could Kill: The Kearny Street hill that takes you up to Telegraph Hill Boulevard. There's no avoiding this one.

Rising sharply from the streets of neighboring North Beach is Telegraph Hill, named for the semaphore that was installed at its peak in 1850 to alert the city to ships' arrivals. The whole city would stop when the semaphore raised its arms to signal that the Pacific Mail Steamship Company's side-wheeler was on its way. Hubert Howe Bancroft, a pioneer bookseller, wrote in his eight-volume history of California that "when the signal flag was unfurled, and the windmill-looking indicator on Telegraph Hill stretched forth its long ungainly wooden arms and told the town of a steamer outside, a thrill went through the heart."

In the 1850s, in addition to the semaphore, the hill was home to many of the city's criminals, but the Vigilance Committee eventually ran them out of town. Later, when the gold rush was in full swing, Chilean and Peruvian groups claimed the hill as home, followed later by the Irish who, when they moved to the Mission District, were supplanted by the Italians.

The fire of 1906 came swiftly to Telegraph Hill, and legend has it that the efforts of some of the Italian residents to douse the flames with 500 barrels of red wine–soaked blankets and burlap bags saved many of the homes on the hill. Because they were able to save their homes, most people living on Telegraph Hill thought they were safe—until 4 months later when the Gray brothers began dynamiting their property to quarry rock out of the hill (the rock was used as ballast for outgoing ships, as well as for street paving and for landfill for building The Embarcadero). The blasts shook the entire hill and lopped off portions of some hill dwellers' lots. Residents were furious, and some tried to take legal action to stop the brothers. The battle dragged on; finally, George Gray was killed by one of his former employees, and that was the end of quarrying on the hill.

Well before the shooting of George Gray, residents were interested in preserving Telegraph Hill, but it wasn't until the 1920s that the Park Commission made an effort in that direction. The road leading to the top of the hill was paved, and an incredibly ugly balustrade punctuated with giant urns (which only served to block the beautiful view) was erected alongside the road. Once again, residents came together in a fury, and the Park Commission was forced to remove the balustrade.

Between the time the Park Commission took the balustrade down and 1933, when Coit Tower was erected,

Telegraph Hill became a haven for artists. They were attracted to the hill because it was an inexpensive and beautiful place to live, and they loved it in spite of (and probably because of) the fact that they had to live in wooden shacks and studio apartments. Some people referred to Telegraph Hill during this time as the "Montparnasse of the West." Like most other artists' communities, this one was discovered by a group of "wannabes," and Telegraph Hill became the trendy place to live in the mid-1930s. The artists, who couldn't afford the new, higher rents, were driven out.

Today, Telegraph Hill has its share of ugly apartment buildings, but it has been able to retain some of its charm, and as you begin this tour in North Beach, you'll pass some of the oldest houses on the hill, climbing wooden steps and walking the wooden boardwalks of Napier Lane. You'll also go into Coit Tower, where you can admire the view and the murals within. Finally, you'll end up at Levi Strauss Plaza, where the jeans company is headquartered.

This walk has a lot of steps and descents, so proceed only when you're feeling well rested.

• • • • • • • • • • • • • • • • •

Exit Washington Square through the intersection of Union and Stockton streets. Head east on Union Street (with the square at your back) to Grant Avenue. Go right on Grant and begin this tour with a little shopping, snacks, and suds on:

1. **Grant Avenue.** This section of Grant is host to the best women's boutique shopping in the city; the 2-block shopping area is so condensed you can't miss it. If you shop now, however, consider returning later for your purchases; you don't want to drag them along with you on this jaunt.

    Continuing along Grant Avenue, duck into as many shops as you like, but consider finishing the street with a cool brew at **The Saloon** (1232 Grant Ave.), whose swinging doors have been greeting patrons since 1861. Not much seems to have changed since that time, including the top-notch music, which culminates with a serious blues jam every Friday, Saturday, and Sunday from 4 to 8pm and 9:30pm to 1:30am.

When you've finished browsing on Grant Avenue, turn around and head back to Green Street. Go right to:

2. **377 Green St.,** the former home of Kenneth Patchen (1911–72) and his wife, Miriam. Patchen was born in Ohio and educated in Arkansas. He started out as a poet, incorporating jazz rhythms and phrasing into his verse. He is credited with being the first poet to experiment along those lines. He also was a painter, and he often designed the covers for his books of poetry. His drawings and paintings have a whimsical, childlike quality about them.

Backtrack to Kearny Street and turn right. After you cross Union Street, you will come to:

3. **1425 Kearny St.,** where Richard Brautigan (1935–84), the Californian author of *Trout Fishing in America* (1967) and *In Watermelon Sugar* (1968), is said to have lived at the end of the 1960s. The story has it that while he was in residence, he decorated the toilet seat with paintings of trout.

After you pass the former Brautigan house, continue up this monster of a hill to the steps that will take you to Telegraph Hill Boulevard. After you catch your breath at the top of the stairs, go right along Telegraph Hill Boulevard, following it until you get to:

4. **Coit Tower,** the white, fluted pillar that was constructed after the death of Lillie Hitchcock Coit with money she had left to the city of San Francisco. She stated in her will that the money was "to be expended in an appropriate manner for the purpose of adding to the beauty of the city which I have always loved." She didn't leave any other specific instructions.

In 1931, after the balustrade fiasco described at the beginning of this chapter, it was decided that Lillie Coit's money would be used to construct a memorial tower on Telegraph Hill, and the view from the top of the tower was not to be obscured by any other building. This would

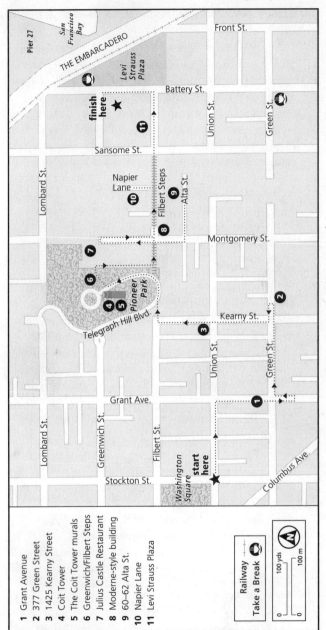

1 Grant Avenue
2 377 Green Street
3 1425 Kearny Street
4 Coit Tower
5 The Coit Tower murals
6 Greenwich/Filbert Steps
7 Julius Castle Restaurant
8 Moderne-style building
9 60–62 Alta St.
10 Napier Lane
11 Levi Strauss Plaza

Railway
Take a Break

Lillie Coit

Lillie Hitchcock Coit (1844–1929) came to San Francisco from Maryland at the age of 7. Soon after arriving in the city, she was a victim of one of the first fires San Francisco ever saw. Lillie was able to escape, but her friends were not. The fire and the deaths of her friends had a lasting effect on her, and when she was a teenager, Coit happened to pass the Knickerbocker Engine Company No. 5 of the Volunteer Fire Department, on their way up Telegraph Hill to douse a fire. Realizing that they could use an extra pair of hands, Lillie dropped her schoolbooks and called all the men within earshot to help her as she began pulling the towrope. Because of her help, Engine No. 5 was the first to get to the top of Telegraph Hill.

The volunteer firemen from Engine No. 5 were so impressed with her that they made her their mascot. From that day onward she would race with them to fires, and in parades she always rode on top of the Knickerbocker engine. In 1863, they made her an honorary member and gave her a diamond-studded badge with "No. 5" written on it. After that, she embroidered

ensure the preservation of Telegraph Hill that residents had been seeking. Because they had only $125,000 to devote to the construction of the memorial, they had to use inexpensive building materials. The cheapest at that time was reinforced concrete.

Many criticized the plan for the tower, saying that it was ugly. Even the author Gertrude Atherton, a friend of Lillie Hitchcock Coit, argued against the memorial, stating that Coit particularly despised towers. Four hundred sixty-four people signed a petition against the building of the tower. Nonetheless, it was built, and it stands today at 212 feet.

In spite of the fact that the tower seems to resemble the nozzle of a fire hose, the architects, Henry Howard and the number five on all her clothing, signed her name Lillie Hitchcock 5, and always attended the annual firemen's banquet.

Lillie married Howard Coit in 1868, and in spite of the fact that he came from a rich Connecticut family, she continued to attend functions with the firemen of Engine No. 5. You might wonder how she behaved at elegant social functions. The answer? The same way she did when she played poker and smoked with her buddies at the fire department, of course. (She also was an excellent shot.)

When her husband died in 1885, Lillie moved away from San Francisco for a time. She returned to the city in 1924 at age 83 and remained here until her death in 1929. Engine No. 5, of course, was present at her funeral; she was even cremated wearing her diamond-studded "No. 5" badge. In her will, she endowed one-third of her estate to the San Francisco Board of Supervisors "for the purpose of adding to the beauty of the city," which, in turn, used the gift to construct the now famous Coit Tower.

Arthur Brown, Jr., claim that the resemblance was never intended. One of the city's many enigmas is that the bronze statue of three firemen and a damsel in distress— erected in 1933 to honor San Francisco's firemen at the bequest of Lillie Hitchcock Coit—ended up in Washington Square facing Columbus Avenue, whereas Coit Tower is fronted by a statue of Christopher Columbus.

Head up to the top for the spectacular 360-degree view of the city from the observation deck. The fee for the ride up the creaky elevator is $3.75 for adults, $2.50 for seniors 64 and over, and $1.50 for kids 6 to 12.

After you descend from the observation deck, take a look at:

5. **The Coit Tower murals.** Soon after Lillie Hitchcock Coit died, the Depression hit, and with the New Deal came government-sponsored projects to help artists and writers survive. The Public Works Art Project (PWAP), a pilot program for the Works Projects Administration (WPA) that was to emerge a year later, commissioned artists to paint, among other things, frescoes (or murals) on the walls of public or government buildings. After Coit Tower was built, it was designated a recipient of this artwork.

Although they numbered close to 30, the artists who worked on Coit Tower were a fairly unified group. Several of them had been students of Mexican muralist Diego Rivera, who also was a political radical with strong ties to Russian Communists. It is in his favored form—the traditional Mexican-style fresco—that the murals were painted, and it is likely that several of the artists sympathized with his politics, too.

The very medium they chose to work in required that they collaborate on both their palette and the scale of their work. Because the technique of fresco requires the hand mixing of a range of earth tones, the palette had to be agreed upon before work began. Only one assistant was given the privilege of grinding and mixing the pigments, simply to ensure the uniformity of color. And the consistent scale was important because if some artists worked on large figures while others worked on miniatures, the individual murals would not have formed a cohesive unit, essential in a building such as Coit Tower, which has no separate rooms.

As you enter the tower, directly ahead you will see the first mural, *Animal Force and Machine Force,* by Ray Boynton. It measures 10 feet by 36 feet and displays both rural (to the left of the door) and urban (to the right of the door) scenes of California. In 1917, Boynton, a professor of art at the University of California at Berkeley, became one of the first artists to work with the fresco medium in San Francisco. This mural includes one of the most interesting, almost mystical features of all the murals in the tower—the eyes of "Old Man Weather" above the doorway.

Go to the right and turn around so that you're looking at the wall by the entrance. This mural, *California Industrial Scenes,* was created by John Langley Howard, who once was a member of the Art Students' League in New York. This is his only known fresco.

As you continue around, you'll find William Hesthal's *Railroad and Shipping* fresco, which attempts to show the effects of the New Deal on the depressed economy of the 1930s. Hesthal was a student of the California School of Fine Arts, and some of his works are housed at the San Francisco Museum of Fine Arts.

The Surveyor and *The Steelworker,* by Clifford Wight, are located on each side of the windows on the wall to your right. Unfortunately, it is now impossible to see the impact that Wight originally had on Coit Tower, because his Communist slogan (which caused the tower to be closed during the summer of 1934) has since been erased. The controversy came about over a piece of cable bent to look like a sickle, a hammer, and the slogan "Workers of the World Unite," the universal symbol of Communism.

On the left you'll see Ralph Stackpole's *Industries of California.* Stackpole was the teacher of Frederick Law Olmsted and a student of the Ecole des Beaux-Arts in Paris. Stackpole once said that he would like to see San Francisco dubbed "The City of Frescoes." Notice the view of the Golden Gate Bridge and Hyde Street Pier behind you.

The next mural, *Newsgathering,* was done by Suzanne Scheuer. This fresco involves some intricately painted elements, among them the painting of the newspaper on the window ledge and the depiction of the color process of making a comic strip (around the window). The painting shows the making of a newspaper from editorial to the printing and selling of the latest edition. You'll probably notice that this painting is a bit brighter than the first few you saw; that's because Scheuer had a greater preference for reds and blues than the other artists.

In the same corner, on the other wall, is a painting of the inside of the public library by Bernard B. Zakheim, a Polish immigrant who came to San Francisco seeking political asylum. He studied at the Mark Hopkins Art Institute (now the San Francisco Art Institute) and painted his first fresco at the Jewish Community Center. He was instrumental in organizing the Coit Tower project.

The next two panels on either side of the windows, by Mallett Dean, depict a stockbroker (some think it's A. P. Giannini; see Walking Tour 3, stop 3, for details) and a scientist. Dean studied at the California School of Fine Arts and worked for many years as a label designer in the California wine industry. Some of his work is housed at the San Francisco Museum of Art.

Turn around to the wall facing the windows, and you'll find yourself transported into a street scene titled *City Life* by Victor Arnautoff. Arnautoff spent 30 years in the United States and studied under Diego Rivera. The intersection shown here is that of Montgomery and Washington streets.

George Harris is responsible for the painting of the next panel to your right as you continue to walk around, which is titled *Banking and the Law.* Some of the titles on the books in the law library are very amusing. Harris attended the California School of Fine Arts and was one of the youngest of the Coit Tower artists.

The adjacent panel is called *Department Store,* executed by Frede Vidar. Born in Denmark but transplanted to San Francisco in 1923 at the age of 12, he studied at the California School of Fine Arts and once had the good fortune of studying with Matisse while in Paris in 1933. The department store scene depicted here is typical of the 1930s, with soda fountain and all.

As you approach the next group of windows, you'll be passing into the agriculture section of the tower, and you'll be greeted by Clifford Wight's *Farmer and Cowboy.* Wight, who also painted *The Surveyor* and *The Steelworker,* is thought to have been a student of Diego Rivera.

Another woman artist, Maxine Albro, painted *California,* the fresco opposite the windows. Also a student of Diego Rivera, she studied at the California School of Fine Arts before leaving for Mexico to study with Rivera. Unfortunately, a lot of her work has been destroyed, but happily, this apricot-, orange-, and flower-picking agricultural scene survives.

In the final corner you'll find Ray Bertrand's *Meat Industry* mural, whose gray tones and flesh colors are in direct contrast to the vibrant, brightly colored outdoor scene that you just saw. Bertrand, a native San Franciscan, also was a student at the California School of Fine Arts, and most of his work consisted of lithography and landscape painting.

The final mural of note here is adjacent to Bertrand's mural and is titled *California Agricultural Industry*. The artist, Gordon Langdon, linked his mural's subject matter with Bertrand's because of their proximity. On one side you see the meatpacking industry, and here you see the actual farm where the animals are raised. Note the man in the silo peeking out the window.

Head back out to the circular parking area. Walk east toward the Bay Bridge and look for the small brick staircase leading down the hill, called the:

6. **Greenwich/Filbert Steps.** This narrow, shaded flight of steps is one of the city's most charming spots, but watch your footing or you'll take a nasty tumble. As you walk down the brick steps, you'll see a cement pathway to your right. Take this pathway, which makes a gentle curve to San Francisco's beloved Filbert Steps. Down the east side of Telegraph Hill, the terrain becomes so steep that Filbert Street becomes Filbert Steps.

Wend your way down the wooden steps bejeweled with beautifully landscaped gardens, thick evergreens, and sweet smells from the profusion of flowers. After you've passed several Victorian and Carpenter Gothic homes (no. 228, built in the 1870s, is a prime example), you'll come to a sort of landing that is actually the upper level of Montgomery Street.

At the bottom of the steps look left, toward the Golden Gate Bridge to see:

7. **Julius Castle Restaurant,** at 1541 Montgomery St. Built in 1921, this cliff-hanging establishment is better appreciated for its view than its food (it's always a top

contender among readers' polls for "Most Romantic" and "Best View," and only open for dinner). The restaurant used to have a turntable out front for automobiles, because it was too difficult to turn a car around at this particular point on Montgomery Street. Since then, the street has been widened, but not by much, and nervous drivers sometimes may wish the turntable were still in operation.

Cross Montgomery Street to the lower level of its hairpin turn to get the best view of the:

8. **Moderne-style building** at 1360 Montgomery St. Built in 1936, this private four-story apartment house was one of the filming locations for Bogie and Bacall's *Dark Passage* (notice Humphrey in the window), as well as *The Maltese Falcon*. Hiram Johnson, the former governor of California, once lived here. Note the exterior murals and handsome glass-block facade leading to the entrance lobby.

Continue south on the lower level of Montgomery Street and head on to Alta Street. Turn left on Alta Street to:

9. **60–62 Alta St.,** the former home of author Armistead Maupin. Originally from Raleigh, North Carolina, Maupin began his career as an author through a serial story in the *San Francisco Chronicle* in 1976. The series of articles was called "Tales of the City" and was widely followed by San Franciscans and out-of-towners who obtained their copies of the story from their San Franciscan friends. Many readers thought they saw themselves in the stories because it was widely known that Maupin based the tales in part on his own experiences in San Francisco's social scene.

From Anna Madrigal, the pot-smoking/growing landlady of 28 Barbary Lane (a fictional lane in San Francisco); to Mary Ann Singleton, a particularly naive Midwesterner who heads for San Francisco to get away from her small-town friends and family; to Michael Tolliver (or Mouse), a gay man in search of true love, Maupin takes us through his characters' lives (and, in turn, our own) as he weaves his splendidly comical tales.

Maupin gathered all his 1976 stories together, and the revised and edited tales were issued as one volume, *Tales of the City.* He followed that volume with another, *More Tales of the City,* and another, *Further Tales of the City.* After that, the titles changed a little bit, but many of the same characters remained. The final three struck a more serious chord with the onset of AIDS. They were *Babycakes, Sure of You,* and finally, *Significant Others.* The first book has been adapted for television as a PBS series.

If you follow Alta Street to the end, you'll find yourself precariously perched at the edge of a precipice, so if you're afraid of heights, don't go. However, you'll be treated to a spectacular vista if you do.

When you're finished admiring the view, go back out to Montgomery Street and go right back to the second half of the Filbert Steps. Turn right and continue down the wooden steps. The second alley on your left is:

10. **Napier Lane,** which probably is one of the only short boardwalk alleys left in the entire city. It is thought that at one time sailors were shanghaied here. On the corner of Napier Lane, at 222 Filbert St., there once was a grocery store and a saloon. You're sure to see many cats wandering the boardwalk, and quite a few more as you continue to descend the Filbert Steps.

    Continue down the Filbert Steps. As you head down the last set of steps, which turn to concrete, you'll see at your right a cliff-side area that looks as if it's under construction. A former rock quarry, this area proved to be quite profitable for excavation, but after a couple of houses fell off the cliff into the pit, excavation had to be stopped.

    When you get to the bottom of the stairs, go straight, crossing Sansome Street into:

11. **Levi Strauss Plaza,** where you'll find the headquarters for Levi Strauss & Co., which was founded in San Francisco. Built in 1982 by Hellmuth, Obata & Kassabaum, this sprawling brick complex was designed to blend in as unobtrusively as possible with the lower slope of Telegraph Hill while complementing the existing brick edifices.

If you go inside the building on your right, you can see exhibits that include designs of old Levi's jeans, including some examples of the first pairs ever made. Ever notice the initials *SF* on the rivets of Levi's jeans? They stand for San Francisco. Another interesting note about the rivets on Levi's jeans is that originally they were put there in an effort to extend the life of the pants. The first work pants designed by Levi's were made for miners whose heavy pockets (loaded with the fruits of their labors) ripped all too often. The rivets strengthened the pockets and were not intended as decorative features.

Winding Down After you exit the corporate head-quarters, cross the street, go left, and on the other side of the plaza, you'll find one of San Francisco's most unusual-looking restaurants—the **Fog City Diner,** at 1300 Battery St.

Now more popular because of its starring role in a Visa commercial a few years ago than for its food today, Fog City is a popular tourist destination, with a few locals straggling in for a business lunch. The restaurant looks like a genuine American metallic diner—but only from the outside. Inside, dark polished woods, inspired lighting, and a well-stocked raw bar tell you this is no hash-slinger. Dressed-up dishes include gourmet crab cakes, salads, sandwiches, burgers, pork chops, and pot roast. If your heart is set on coming here, do so at lunch; but if you want a truly special lunch or dinner you'll be better off heading to **Piperade,** which is located a few blocks south at 1015 Battery St. at Green Street. If you're coming for lunch, keep in mind it's only open midday during weekdays.

From here, the no. 10 bus goes north on Sansome to the intersection of Powell and North Point streets, from where you can either walk 7 blocks south on Powell to Washington Square or transfer to the no. 39 bus, which heads directly to Washington Square; be sure to ask the driver for a free transfer.

The Haughty Hotels of Nob Hill

Walking Tour 5

Start: Corner of Taylor and California streets.

Public Transportation: Bus: Take the no. 1 bus to Taylor and Sacramento streets and walk 1 block over to California Street; cable car: Take the California Line to the corner of Taylor and California streets.

Finish: Corner of Taylor and Clay streets.

Time: 2 hours.

Best Times: Between 10am and 5pm.

Worst Times: Before 10am or after 5pm.

Hills That Could Kill: Do not climb up Jones or Taylor streets between Bush and California streets unless you're fond of sweating. The block of Taylor between Pine and California streets has a 23.7% grade, so if you're looking for a particularly good workout, go on up (if you need to rest, you can just lean against the hill).

R ising 338 feet above sea level and bounded roughly by Pine, Pacific, Stockton, and Polk streets, Nob Hill is one of the highest and best known of San Francisco's many hills.

In the beginning it was well known only because of its height, and was occupied by the poor because the rich didn't want to climb the treacherously sandy hill to reach their homes. So, instead of the mansions you see today, a series of wooden shacks dotted the hill in the early 1800s.

Beginning in the 1850s, a few more prosperous merchants and doctors sought refuge from the turmoil of life on Montgomery Street. The first person to build a permanent home on the hill was a doctor by the name of Arthur Hayne. He was followed by Senator George Hearst (father of William Randolph Hearst) and a merchant by the name of William Walton.

Hallidie's invention of the cable car in the 1870s (San Francisco's golden era) made the hills much more accessible, and those first forward-looking residents soon were followed by a long line of millionaires who recognized the potential value of the real estate atop the hill. They included, among others, the Big Four (Crocker, Hopkins, Huntington, and Stanford) who built the Central (later Southern) Pacific Railroad, and the Bonanza Kings (O'Brien, Flood, Fair, and Mackay) who struck it rich with the Comstock Lode. They were the "nabobs" who gave Nob Hill its name.

The original Big Four began making their money as shopkeepers who sold supplies to the miners during the gold rush. Leland Stanford had been a grocer in Sacramento, Charlie Crocker was a dry-goods clerk, and Collis P. Huntington and Mark Hopkins sold hardware. At heart, they were simple men who wanted to lead simple lives. Then, with the building of the railroad in 1869, they struck it rich—*really* rich.

In 1876, after they decided to move to Nob Hill, the Stanfords set about building an elaborate Italian villa, which included the largest private dining room in the West. Mark Hopkins preferred less ostentatious digs, but his wife, 20 years his junior, worked her charms on him until he gave her carte blanche to design whatever she desired. The result was a palatial estate adorned with Gothic spires, wooden towers, and elaborate ornamentation. (In a twist of fate, Hopkins died before the house was completed, leaving his wife to finish the job; she then married the interior decorator.) Crocker also built an ornate mansion that stood on the site of present-day Grace Cathedral. Huntington and Flood also built mansions of their own. "Bonanza Jim" Fair, though, never completed his planned mansion on the hill—his marriage ended in divorce before he got the chance.

Shortly after the mansions were completed, the 1906 earthquake and fire destroyed all except the Flood Mansion, parts of which still stand today. Some of the nabobs rebuilt; others left. Crocker's family donated his lot to the Episcopal Church for the building of a cathedral (now Grace Cathedral). Later, in the 1920s, some of the new mansions were converted into hotels, and Grace Cathedral's construction began. With the later construction of some high-rise apartment buildings, the hill lost some of its reputation as "Snob Hill," and many middle-class people now live on the sloping sides of the hill (the top, replete with high-class hotels, is still reserved for the wealthy, however).

This tour begins at the summit of Nob Hill and slowly descends the northwestern slope of the hill. You'll see the famed Grace Cathedral and walk by the Flood Mansion. You'll also visit the ostentatious Mark Hopkins and Fairmont hotels, ending the tour at the marvelous Cable Car Barn and Museum.

If you're feeling particularly energetic, you might want to tie this tour onto the Russian Hill tour, so we have included walking directions to the starting point of the Russian Hill tour at the end of this one.

● ● ● ● ● ● ● ● ● ● ● ● ● ● ● ● ●

On the corner of Taylor and California streets, you'll see the massive:

1. **Grace Cathedral,** which stands on the site of the old Charles Crocker mansion. Crocker was among the first group of millionaires to build on Nob Hill, and, like Mark Hopkins's wife, Crocker stuffed his redwood

château full of treasures from Europe, including such items as Millet's *The Sower*. He had assembled the lot piecemeal, but there was still a corner owned and occupied by an undertaker named Mr. Yung. Yung saw how much Crocker wanted the land, and when Crocker asked him to sell, he demanded an exorbitant sum. Instead of giving in to Mr. Yung's demands, an enraged Crocker built a 40-foot-high "spite fence," depriving Yung of sunlight in an attempt to drive his price down. The dispute wasn't settled until after the deaths of both men (the Yung family eventually sold the property), but it mattered little because both estates were destroyed by the fire that swept the hill in 1906. Not long after the fire, the Crocker family donated the land to the Episcopal diocese.

The original Grace Church stood at the intersection of Powell and Jackson streets and was built in 1849 under the direction of Reverend Dr. John L. Ver Mehr, a Belgian who was the first Episcopal priest in San Francisco. Many of the first parishioners were miners, and when the collection plate was passed, they often filled it with gold dust. Later, a bigger church was built at the intersection of Stockton and California streets and was occupied by Bishop Kip, the first bishop of California. The 1906 earthquake and fire destroyed the church, and because it was well known before the fire that the new bishop, Bishop Nichols, wanted to build a cathedral on a hill, the Crocker family donated their land.

Plans were drawn up for a new cathedral in 1907, and the cornerstone was laid and dedicated 3 years later. However, work on the present structure didn't begin until 1928. Lewis P. Hobart worked 3 years designing this primarily French Gothic cathedral on a cross-shaped plan, but he died 10 years before its completion in 1964. Although the cathedral looks like it's made of stone, in fact, it is constructed of reinforced concrete, which was beaten to achieve a stonelike effect.

Grace Cathedral is the third-largest Episcopal cathedral in the country, and when you survey it, you'll want to look for several outstanding features. Its main doors are stunning replicas of Ghiberti's bronze Doors of Paradise

Nob Hill

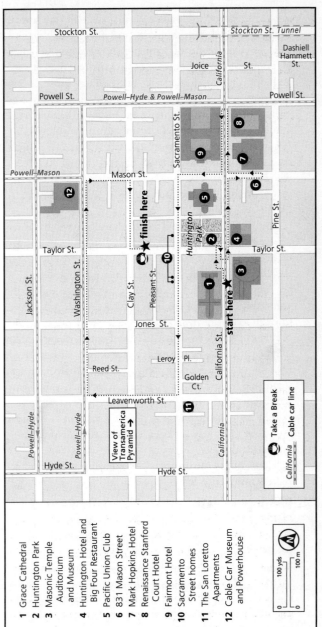

Stockton St.

Stockton St. Tunnel

Joice

California St.

Dashiell
Hammett
St.

Powell St.

Powell–Hyde & Powell–Mason

Powell St.

Sacramento St.

8

Powell–Mason

Mason St.

9

7

finish here ★

5

6

Pine St.

Taylor St.

10

Huntington
Park

2

4

Taylor St.

Jackson St.

Washington St.

Clay St.

Pleasant St.

1

3

start here ★

Jones St.

Leroy Pl.

Reed St.

Golden
Ct.

Powell–Hyde

Powell–Hyde

Leavenworth St.

11

California

View of
Transamerica
Pyramid →

Take a Break

Hyde St.

Hyde St.

California

Cable car line

N

100 yds
100 m

0
0

1 Grace Cathedral
2 Huntington Park
3 Masonic Temple
  Auditorium
  and Museum
4 Huntington Hotel and
  Big Four Restaurant
5 Pacific Union Club
6 831 Mason Street
7 Mark Hopkins Hotel
8 Renaissance Stanford
  Court Hotel
9 Fairmont Hotel
10 Sacramento
   Street homes
11 The San Loretto
   Apartments
12 Cable Car Museum
   and Powerhouse

in the Baptistery in Florence. Inside, you will find several brilliant stained-glass windows and a series of religious frescoes. One group of stained-glass windows, designed by Loire Studios of Chartres, depicts such modern figures as Judge Thurgood Marshall, poet Robert Frost (a San Francisco native), Albert Einstein, and John Dewey, as well as many others. The frescoes, referred to as the World Church Murals, are by Polish-American artist John H. De Rosen and were painted in the late 1940s. The organ dates from 1860, and David Lemon created its Hosea wood sculpture. The Singing Tower (to the right of the main entrance) was given its name because of its incredible 44-bell carillon.

There also is a carpeted labyrinth in the nave that is set on canvas and edged in purple lines. A sign asks that shoes be laid outside the entrance, thus footfalls are silent and the carpet unmarked. It's an odd sensation to walk within the labyrinth's bounds, with your feet feeling unusually vulnerable outside the confines of your shoes as you swerve through folds and switchbacks. Its plan is identical to that of one in the cathedral at Chartres, France, where monks use the path to contemplate. It's a fixed path, with no dead ends or diverging routes, only a center where you can stand and think before you return to trace your steps again.

The cathedral generally is open from about 7:30am to 6 or 7pm every day, and you can visit the gift shop during the day.

Come out of the cathedral the way you entered and go right across Taylor Street to:

2. **Huntington Park,** a public oasis in the midst of San Francisco's most prestigious hotels. The park is framed by granite walls that once were a part of the Colton estate. David Colton, who has never been adequately recognized for his part in the building of the Central (Southern) Pacific Railroad, perhaps is best known for his role in the Great Diamond Hoax of 1871 (see "The Great Diamond Hoax of 1871," below).

The faux-marble Colton mansion was burned in the fire that followed the 1906 earthquake. Huntington, who had

The Great Diamond Hoax of 1871

In 1871 two roughneck miners, Mr. Arnold and Mr. Slack, deposited two bags of what they said were rough-cut diamonds in the Bank of California. Mr. Ralston, the treasurer of the bank, sought them out and persuaded them to sell him a half-share of the mine. Ralston also asked for the right to inspect the property. Arnold and Slack agreed only if the inspectors could be blindfolded when they got close to the mine entrance so that the location of the find would remain a secret. Ralston agreed to be blindfolded, and he chose David Colton, who then worked for the Southern Pacific Railroad, as the inspector.

Colton inspected the mine, returning to Ralston trembling with excitement, and poured several jewels out onto the table before his employer. Colton explained that there were so many stones that all he had done was simply bend over and gather them up. The gems were genuine, and a respected mining engineer, Henry Janin, confirmed the value of the mines. Thus, Ralston organized a syndicate, establishing the North American Diamond Company. David Colton was appointed its general manager, resigning his executive position at the Southern Pacific Railroad.

News of the diamond find traveled, kindling excitement and curiosity. Scientist and scholar Clarence King was so curious that he set out to visit the mines and found anthills powdered with emerald dust that contained emeralds within, and diamonds in the forks of tree branches. Finally he discovered a partially cut diamond—the mine had been salted! He wired Ralston the news that the mines were a fraud.

Slack disappeared, and Arnold returned to Kentucky with the $300,000 that had been paid to him by Ralston and other shareholders, later becoming a banker. Ralston paid back the investors in the diamond business and absorbed a $300,000 personal loss. He later stretched himself so thin financially that he lost all his money. In 1875, his body—an apparent suicide—was found bobbing around in San Francisco Bay.

purchased the property from Colton in 1892, donated the
land to the city after the burned-out lot had stood empty
for 9 years.

The fountain at the center of the park is said to be a
replica of Italy's Tartarughe Fountain in Rome, commissioned by Pope Alexander VII and erected in 1581. Note
the Dancing Sprites sculpture.

On the opposite corner of California Street, facing the
Grace Cathedral, is the:

3. **Masonic Temple Auditorium and Museum,** which
is at 1111 California St. It's the off-white stone building
at the southwest corner of California and Taylor streets.
The cornerstone, which contains a copper casket with historical Masonic and contemporary documents, was dedicated on September 29, 1958.

Before you go inside, note the bas-relief on the left side
of the building. The four figures to the left represent each
branch of the armed forces; the smaller figures represent
"a global struggle between the forces of good and evil."
The work is dedicated to "Our Masonic Brethren Who
Died in the Cause of Freedom."

Enter the building by ascending the short flight of
steps between the white marble pillars, and directly ahead
you'll see the dramatic 45-by-48-foot Endo-Mosaic window, which is made primarily of plastic instead of glass
and depicts the history of California Masonry. On the
right side of the window are eight vignettes that show
scenes from 1840 to the present. In the center are two
groupings, the seafarers and wayfarers, representing the
two groups that came to California in the 1800s. One of
the most important symbols in Freemasonry is the all-see-
ing eye (which is depicted on the dollar bill); it is featured
at the top of the mural.

Upstairs you'll find some historic Masonic articles on
display.

As you leave the temple, turn right on California Street
and cross Taylor Street. On the corner are the:

4. **Huntington Hotel and Big Four Restaurant,** 1075
California St., named for railroad magnate Collis P.

Huntington. One of the kings of Nob Hill, the stately Huntington Hotel has long been a favorite retreat for Hollywood stars and political VIPs who desire privacy and security. Family-owned since 1924—and thus a real rarity among large hotels—the Huntington eschews pomp and circumstance; absolute privacy and unobtrusive service are its mainstay. Although the lobby, decorated in a grand 19th-century style, is rather petite, the guest rooms—no two of which are alike—are quite large and feature Brunschwig and Fils fabrics and bed coverings, antique French furnishings, and extraordinary views of the city.

The Big Four Restaurant is named for Huntington and his three partners: Hopkins, Stanford, and Crocker. The restaurant is decorated with period furnishings that date back to San Francisco's golden era: shining brass fixtures, historic California photographs, forest-green leather banquettes, ram's horn sconces, and the like. Skip dinner here—there are plenty of better high-end options, but do drop by for a nightcap to see what the Big Four railroad tycoons considered high fashion back then.

When you exit the hotel, turn right, continuing down California Street. Just past Huntington Park on your left is the:

5. **Pacific Union Club,** 1000 California St. Built in 1886 of Connecticut brownstone, this was the original James Flood mansion. Because it was built of stone and not wood, it was one of the few mansions atop Nob Hill to survive the fire of 1906 (although the interior was gutted, the stone foundation weathered the catastrophe). It was remodeled from 1908 to 1912 by Willis Polk, who added the upper floor and the wings, but the main structure you see today is the original. The bronze fence that surrounds the house is one of the city's most beautiful, and it is told that Flood employed one man just to polish the fence. The original cost of the fence was $30,000.

Unfortunately, the Pacific Union Club is a private club, and the public is not admitted.

Note that across the street at 1001 California St. (right across the street from the Pacific Union Club) is the mansion in which Patty Hearst's parents lived during the time that Patty was kidnapped.

Continue east along California Street and when you reach Mason Street, turn right. Stay to the right side of Mason as you're facing down the hill. Go about halfway down the block to:

6. **831 Mason St.** This is where the novelist Erskine Caldwell (1903–87) lived sometime around 1961. Caldwell was born in Georgia, and his novels, including *Tobacco Road* and *God's Little Acre,* generally were set in the rural south. He was married to Margaret Bourke-White, one of the original photographers at *Life* and *Time* magazines.

Return to the corner of Mason and California streets to the:

7. **Mark Hopkins Hotel,** at 999 California St. One of San Francisco's most opulent mansions once stood here. After Mark Hopkins struck it rich on the railroad, his wife proceeded to build a mansion with towers, turrets, verandas, porticos, and a Gothic glass conservatory. The result was a hodgepodge of styles, a French château with Gothic, Greek, and Arabic details. The mansion's interior was no less ornate; Mrs. Hopkins created an ostentatious display of wealth, exemplified by the decor of the master bedroom, which had ebony walls inlaid with precious stones and ivory.

Mark Hopkins died in 1878, and 15 years later his wife gave their home to the San Francisco Art Institute.

Like many other mansions on Nob Hill, this one burned in the fire of 1906. There are many written accounts of art students fleeing with artwork under their arms, propping canvases against houses that were not yet burning while they rushed in for more.

After the fire, the art institute sold the land and moved to its current location on Russian Hill (for more on the San Francisco Art Institute, see Walk 6, stop 14). In 1926 the 19-story Gothic Revival Mark Hopkins Hotel was erected.

The hotel gained global fame during World War II when it was considered de rigueur for Pacific-bound servicemen to toast their good-bye to the States in the Top of the Mark cocktail lounge. Nowadays, the hotel caters mostly to tourists and convention-bound corporate executives who can afford the high rates. Its rooftop lounge, Top of the Mark, is open to the public and is a popular spot for enjoying an evening cocktail while admiring the stellar views of the city.

Continue along to 950 California St., site of the:

8. **Renaissance Stanford Court Hotel.** The Stanford Court has maintained a long and discreet reputation as one of San Francisco's most exclusive—and expensive— hotels. Holding company with the Ritz, Fairmont, Mark Hopkins, and Huntington hotels atop Nob Hill, it originally was the mansion of Leland Stanford, whose legacy lives on in the many portraits and biographies that adorn the rooms.

Leland Stanford, who was both governor of and U.S. senator from California, studied law in an Albany, New York office and was admitted to the bar in 1848. He married a local Albany girl by the name of Jane Lathrop, and together they went west—first to Wisconsin and then to California, where they built their fortune together. He orchestrated the building of the Central (later Southern) Pacific Railroad, and their marriage was quite harmonious. However, in 1884, tragedy struck when they lost their son to typhoid fever in Florence. Subsequently, Stanford told his wife, "The children of California shall be our children."

Together, in 1886, they endowed Leland Stanford Junior University (still its legal name) in Palo Alto, at an estate they had purchased from George Gordon. The university opened in 1891, but the endowment later was threatened by a growing national financial panic. In 1893, during his effort to keep his university alive, Leland died. Jane continued his work, living frugally and selling off property to save money to support the university. She died in 1905; today, Stanford University consistently ranks among the nation's finest.

If you're at all interested in hotel decor, do go in and take a look because the outside of the building is deceptively plain. The lobby, furnished in a 19th-century theme with Baccarat chandeliers, French antiques, and a gorgeous stained-glass dome, makes for a grand entrance.

Cross to the other side of California Street and retrace your steps to the corner of California and Mason streets opposite the Mark Hopkins Hotel. You're now standing alongside the elegant:

9. **Fairmont Hotel,** 950 Mason St., the granddaddy of Nob Hill's elite cadre of ritzy hotels that was built by Tessie Fair Oelrichs, the daughter of silver magnate James G. Fair. Fair, born in Ireland in 1831, came to the West for the gold rush in 1849. He was one of the original founders and developers of the Comstock Lode but, because of the breakup of his marriage, never built a mansion on Nob Hill like the rest of the bonanza kings.

The decision to dynamite various sections of the city during the 1906 fire was made in the ballroom here and announced by General Frederick Funston. After the fire, the badly damaged hotel was restored by architect Julia Morgan.

Although it's not the most exclusive hotel on the hill, the Fairmont wins top honors for the most awe-inspiring lobby in San Francisco. Be sure to wander around the immense space to gape at the massive marble Corinthian columns, vaulted ceilings, and spectacular wraparound staircase.

As you exit the hotel, go right to the intersection of Mason and Sacramento streets, where the horizon (on both sides) opens to a dramatic vista. Go left on Sacramento, keeping to the left side of the street, so that you can get a good view of three notable:

10. **Sacramento Street homes** on the right side of the street. The first, at 1172 Sacramento St., is a remarkable town house constructed in 1908. If you continue on Sacramento across Taylor Street, you'll find 1230 and

1242 Sacramento St. (also on the right side). These two homes probably are the most aesthetically pleasing of the buildings on this street (even though they exist in the shadow of the big hotels). Both are reminiscent of Parisian architecture with their bay windows and cast-iron balconies. Note the plaster detailing.

As you continue along toward Leavenworth Street, you'll also come across two beautifully maintained alleyways. Look first on your left for Leroy Place, and then look for Golden Court on the same side of the street, just a little farther on.

When you reach Leavenworth Street, you'll see:

11. **The San Loretto Apartments,** straight ahead of you on the southwest corner of Leavenworth. Here, in apartment 2 at 1155 Leavenworth St., was Dashiell Hammett's final address in San Francisco, and it is where he finished his novel *The Maltese Falcon.*

    Go right up Leavenworth Street to Clay Street; you now are at the highest point of Nob Hill. If you look to your right along Clay Street, you'll be able to see the Transamerica Pyramid.

    Continue along Leavenworth Street to Washington Street. Turn right, passing Jones and Taylor streets, to Mason Street. On your left side is the:

12. **Cable Car Museum and Powerhouse.** This fascinating (and free) "museum" is your last stop on the Nob Hill walking tour. Be sure to take your time here.

    Probably more famous than the Transamerica Pyramid or any other landmark in San Francisco is the city's cable car system, and the whole operation is run out of this single building. The cable car system was invented by Andrew Hallidie, a metal-rope manufacturer from England. Hallidie got the idea for the cable car system when he saw a horse and carriage tumble backward down a hill because the hill was too steep and the carriage's load was too heavy.

    The original line only ran from Clay Street down Nob Hill, but the system quickly expanded. (Leland Stanford is responsible for the California Street line because he wanted to be delivered to his front door every evening.) As the cable car system grew, areas of the city that had previously been inaccessible by horse and wagon—and too steep for people to climb—were developed.

Before the 1906 earthquake and fire, the cable car system was running 600 different cars, but it, too, suffered great damage during that disaster. After the quake, the system was never the same again. Today, the system runs only three lines, which underwent a $60-million restoration project in 1984. They've been registered as a National Historic Landmark since 1964 and are here to stay.

Go inside the Cable Car Barn, first to the underground viewing room where you can see each of the single cables that runs the cable cars. There are brief written explanations outside each area, so you can really get a grip on what you're looking at. The museum has a gift shop that sells books, postcards, and various cable car reproductions. The museum is open daily April through September from 10am to 6pm and October through March from 10am to 5pm; it is closed major holidays.

Your tour ends here, but if you're ready for lunch, there's a lovely little eatery located at 1148 Taylor St., the Nob Hill Café. From the Cable Car Museum, go right on Mason to Clay Street. Go right again on Clay, then left on Taylor Street (yes, you'll be ready to sit down by the time you get there).

Winding Down Considering the cost and formality of most meals on ultra-elite Nob Hill, it's no wonder neighborhood residents often willingly wait for a table to open up at the **Nob Hill Café,** 1148 Taylor St. This is the kind of place where you can come wearing jeans, relax over a large bowl of pasta and a glass of sangiovese, and leave fulfilled without blowing a wad of dough. The dining area is split into two small, simple rooms, with windows looking onto Taylor Street and bright local art on the walls. Service is friendly, and one of the owners is almost always on hand to keep everyone satisfied. When the kitchen is "on," expect fare worth at least twice its price; on an "off" day, it's still decent. Start with a salad or the decadent polenta with tomato sauce. Then fill up on one of the veal piccata, any of the pastas or pizzas, and petrole sole.

If you're going to couple this tour with the Russian Hill tour (Walking Tour 6), go back to the intersection of Taylor and Clay streets and continue along Taylor (if you're skipping lunch and starting directly from the museum, go left on Taylor St.) to Broadway.

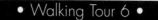

The Ghosts of
Russian Hill

Start: Corner of Broadway and Taylor Street (at the top of the steps).

Public Transportation: Bus: No. 12 will take you within a block of this walk; cable cars: Powell-Mason and Powell-Hyde will take you within a block of this walk.

Finish: Corner of Chestnut and Jones streets.

Time: 2 hours.

Best Times: Tuesday through Saturday between 10am and 5pm.

Worst Times: Sunday and Monday, when the San Francisco Art Institute is closed.

Hills That Could Kill: The steps that lead to the upper level of Broadway from Taylor Street.

Local legend has it that Russian Hill's name is a memento of the visits made by groups of Russian seamen, who came down from Sitka to hunt sea otter for their skins. Those who died on the expeditions apparently were buried on this hill.

Russian Hill was a bohemian center long before Telegraph Hill or North Beach, and while the millionaires were busy sprucing up Nob Hill with mansions, the artists and writers of Russian Hill were living in little shacks and cottages, painting the views, drinking cheap wine, and taking part in intellectual discourse. Today, there's still a small community of writers and artists on the hill, but for the most part they've all been driven to other neighborhoods (such as the Mission District) by rising rents.

This tour will take you by the homes and haunts of famous bohemians, such as Ina Donna Coolbrith and Jack Kerouac. You'll also get a feel for the local color as you pass the homes of Kate Atkinson and Pop Demarest. You'll discover hidden passages with wooden steps, and you'll be charmed by the cottage-style homes at the hill's summit. And, of course, there are the breathtaking views.

● ● ● ● ● ● ● ● ● ● ● ● ● ● ● ●

Begin at the corner of Broadway and Taylor Street. Proceed up the Broadway steps. Your first stop will be at the top:

1. **1032 Broadway,** the former home of Kate Atkinson, who for many years opened her doors to various artists and writers. A group of writers called "Les Jeunes" were among those who gathered here. Nine young, irreverent members made up the group, but by far the most interesting of them was Gelett Burgess.

   Burgess, born in Boston in 1868, received a Bachelor of Science degree from the Massachusetts Institute of Technology before moving to San Francisco, where he worked for Southern Pacific Railway and for the University of California. He made a speedy entrance into the literary world as an editor of a weekly publication called the *Wave*, where he replaced Frank Norris (who had left to complete *McTeague*). It didn't take long for Burgess to found his own publication, the *Lark*.

   Working with the other members of Les Jeunes, Burgess printed the *Lark* on bamboo paper and filled its pages with whatever struck his fancy. Each issue featured a serious poem, essay, and fictional story, but most of its pages were filled with nonsensical rhyming verse. Burgess himself wrote one of the ditties you might recognize:

> *I never Saw a Purple Cow;*
> *I never Hope to See One;*
> *But I can Tell you, Anyhow,*
> *I'd rather See than Be one.*

After its publication in one of the 24 issues of the *Lark* (plus an *Epilark*), the country went mad for it, and it was published and quoted and requoted in thousands of magazines.

Burgess also wrote a wonderful poem titled "The Ballad of the Hyde Street Grip," for which he probably would rather be remembered, so we'll leave one of his favorite hangouts with a stanza from that rhyme:

> *North Beach to Tenderloin, over Russian Hill,*
> *The grades are something giddy, and the curves are fit to kill!*
> *All the way to Market Street, clanging up the slope,*
> *Down upon the other side, clinging to the rope!*
> *But the view of San Francisco, as you take the lurching dip!*
> *There is plenty of excitement on the Hyde Street Grip!*

Directly across the street is:

2. **1051 Broadway,** one of Herb Gold's residences. A former student at New York's Columbia University and classmate of Allen Ginsberg, Gold has lived in San Francisco for more than 30 years. He's a best-selling author whose novels include *Fathers* and *Dreaming*. He contributes regularly to magazines and is well known for his witty essays about San Francisco.

A bit farther on is:

3. **1067 Broadway,** the former home of poet Ina Donna Coolbrith (1842–1928). The niece of Mormon Church founder Joseph Smith, she was born Josephine Smith, the daughter of Joseph's brother, Don Carlos. Coolbrith's father died when she was only 4 months old, and her

Russian Hill

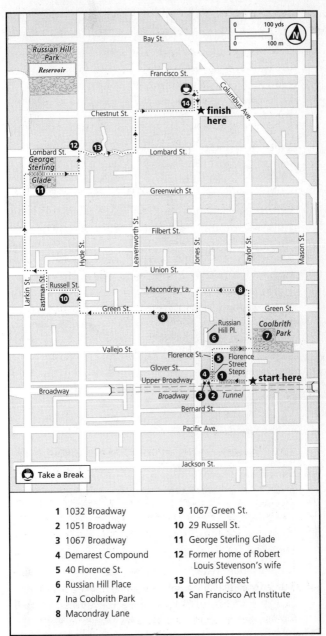

Russian Hill Park
Reservoir

Bay St.

Francisco St.

Columbus Ave

Chestnut St.

★ **finish here**

Lombard St.
George
Sterling
Glade

Lombard St.

Greenwich St.

Filbert St.

Hyde St.

Leavenworth St.

Jones St.

Taylor St.

Mason St.

Union St.

Macondray La.

Russell St.

Larkin St.

Eastman St.

Green St.

Green St.

Russian
Hill Pl.

Coolbrith
Park

Vallejo St.

Florence St.
Glover St.
Upper Broadway

Florence
Street
Steps

★ **start here**

Broadway

Broadway

Tunnel

Bernard St.

Pacific Ave.

Jackson St.

🍴 Take a Break

1	1032 Broadway	**9**	1067 Green St.
2	1051 Broadway	**10**	29 Russell St.
3	1067 Broadway	**11**	George Sterling Glade
4	Demarest Compound	**12**	Former home of Robert Louis Stevenson's wife
5	40 Florence St.	**13**	Lombard Street
6	Russian Hill Place	**14**	San Francisco Art Institute
7	Ina Coolbrith Park		
8	Macondray Lane		

mother, who abandoned Mormonism because she disagreed with polygamy, took Josephine and her two siblings from Nauvoo, Illinois, west to St. Louis. They finally took the epic journey overland to California, stopping first in San Francisco, but finally settling in Los Angeles.

Josephine began writing, and at the age of 11, she had her first poems published in the *Los Angeles Star*. At 17 she married Robert B. Carsley, a minstrel-show performer. Three short and brutal years later, she divorced him and moved to San Francisco, taking the name Ina Donna Coolbrith, under which she had been writing her poetry.

Aside from being a poet, she was an inspiration for writers, poets, artists, and philosophers in early San Francisco and was greatly loved by her contemporaries. She began working with Bret Harte on the *Overland Monthly* (in 1868), but poetry did not pay her bills or support her family, so she took a job in the Oakland Public Library where she worked for more than 25 years. It was in the Oakland library that she met 12-year-old Jack London, then poor, shabbily dressed, and generally uncared for. He was asking for something to read. Coolbrith guided and inspired him, and of her he said, "I loved Ina Coolbrith above all womankind, and what I am and what I have done that is good I owe to her."

In 1915, at the age of 73, she was proclaimed Poet Laureate of California at the University of California.

On the other side of the street, at 1078–1080 Broadway, is the location of what was once known as the:

4. **Demarest Compound.** The old "compound" was really just a small grouping of cottages that was built to house refugees after the earthquake of 1906. After the refugees moved, the cottages, surrounded by shrubs and flowers, were home to many writers, but they no longer exist. However, you can't take a trip to Russian Hill without learning about old Pop Demarest, who built the cottages and owned the land upon which they were built.

Pop Demarest lived up here until he died in 1939, at the age of 87, but he wasn't known to more than a handful of people until his obituary, which called him "The Hermit of Russian Hill," was published. For many years he lived in an abandoned cistern pipe under the buildings at the compound, later moving into the basement of one of the cottages.

Demarest hated to bathe, but he loved to drink, and every month he would go on a drunken binge. For several days he would run naked through the compound gardens, throwing bottles and making a general nuisance of himself. His tenants didn't mind, though; they just locked their doors and waited patiently until he quieted down. His tenants probably were tolerant of this outrageous behavior—in part, at least—because Demarest didn't really care when or if they paid their rent. Money meant nothing to him.

After Demarest died, reporters flocked to his basement room to see what it was like. They found it full of cobwebs, knickknacks, dried animal skins, thousands of records (many by Adelina Patti, whom he was crazy about), photographs, and hordes of hungry cats.

Now head east until you reach the street sign marking Florence Street. It's tucked behind a tree on the north side of the street at the cusp of the hill. Head up the set of stairs on the north side of the road (the Florence St. Steps). When you reach the top of the stairs, you'll be on Florence Street. Look for:

5. **40 Florence Street,** which once was the home of architect Willis Polk (1867–1924). In his early career, Polk spent time working for the firm Van Brunt and Howe in Kansas City, and later for A. Page Brown in New York. When Brown moved his office to San Francisco in 1889, Polk moved with him, and it was here that Polk flourished. His work has been described as "versatile" and "unpredictable," paving the way for many San Francisco architects to come. The tendency to mix and match styles is a technique frequently repeated in San Francisco homes of the Victorian period. Polk built an enormous number of houses and worked on many churches and office buildings during his career. In 1917 he designed the first glass curtain–walled building in the world (the Hallidie Building, at 130–150 Sutter St.).

While he made his living in architecture, Polk still had time to take part in some bohemian escapades. In fact, he was an active member of Les Jeunes and often contributed drawings or architectural essays to some of the magazines of the time, such as Gelett Burgess's *Lark*.

Continue to the end of Florence Street and turn left on Vallejo Street. Across the street you'll see a small lane called:

6. **Russian Hill Place.** Mystery writer Virginia Rath, once a resident of Russian Hill Place, gave one of her characters, Michael Dundas, a home here in the quaint, hidden cul-de-sac that tops Russian Hill.

Born in Colusa County, California, Rath had her primary education in country schools, where she began writing and submitting stories to publishers before she was 16. In 1935, the Crime Club published her first novel, *Death at Dagton's Folly.* Her next few novels made her one of the most popular mystery writers of her time.

Come back out of Russian Hill Place and go left to the end of Vallejo Street, where you'll find—along with a terrific perch on which to soak in the spectacular view of the city and bay—a set of stairs to the right. Go down the stairs, cross Taylor Street, and follow another set of stairs into:

7. **Ina Coolbrith Park.** Coolbrith lived near here on Taylor Street until her apartment burned down in the fire of 1906. In the fire, she lost letters from such friends as Lord Tennyson, Dante Gabriel Rossetti, and Henry Wadsworth Longfellow, and from closer everyday companions such as Mark Twain, Bret Harte, and Charles Warren Stoddard. She met Twain and Stoddard when she worked in the offices of the *Overland Monthly.*

Harte, Stoddard, and Coolbrith enjoyed taking trips to Mount Tamalpais and Muir Woods, and they often drank together in Sausalito or sat in Coolbrith's Russian Hill house reading poetry together. After the fire destroyed the home, friends raised money and purchased two apartments for her, one of which provided enough rental income to meet her living expenses. (***Note:*** Keep an eye and ear out for the flock of wild parakeets that reside here. You can't help but hear their horrible screeching as they zoom overhead.)

Come out of the park the way you entered, and go right on Taylor Street until you come to a wooden staircase on the left side of the street, which is:

8. **Macondray Lane,** the quintessential San Francisco pedestrian street, inaccessible to cars or any other form of transportation. Some people believe that this street was the model for Armistead Maupin's *Barbary Lane,* whereas others believe Filbert Street was (because of its proximity to Maupin's own home). In any case, this is a wonderful street to walk along with its overhanging trees and wandering flowers. You're sure to find several cats hanging out under the steps or near the houses.

   When you come to Jones Street, turn left, and then turn right on Green Street to:

9. **1067 Green St.,** which will be on your left. This octagonal house, better known as the Feusier Octagon, originally was constructed in 1859. Louis Feusier, a San Francisco merchant, added the cupola and mansard roofing 20 or 30 years later. The house was built at a time when it was rumored that people would be healthier if they lived in octagonal spaces, and although it makes for interesting architecture, there was never any proof that this claim was true. A similar octagon-shaped house is located at the corner of Union and Gough streets and now is a museum and home to the National Society of Colonial Dames of America (see stop 16 of Walk 7).

   A bit farther along on the right, at no. 1088, is a Tudor Revival firehouse that dates from 1907 and was designed by Newton J. Tharp. The firehouse was still in use until the early 1950s. It later was purchased and restored by Louise S. Davies, who donated it to the National Trust for Historic Preservation in 1978.

   Continue along Green Street to Hyde Street. Go right on Hyde to Russell Street. Go left to:

10. **29 Russell St.,** where Jack Kerouac lived with Neal Cassady and Neal's wife when he came back to the West Coast in 1952. During his 6-month stay, Kerouac worked on revising *On the Road* and collaborated with Cassady on the art of spontaneous writing. Out of some of their conversations, which were tape-recorded as examples of spontaneity, came several sections of *Visions of Cody.*

If you continue west on Russell Street, you'll come to the intersection of Russell and Eastman streets. Go right here to Union Street, and then go left. When you get to Larkin Street, go right 2½ blocks to the Greenwich Street Steps, which will take you up to the:

11. **George Sterling Glade.** After the suicide of the "King of Bohemia," George Sterling's friends and contemporaries gathered for the dedication of this memorial park. A tiled bench and plaque were installed here, but the bench broke and the plaque was stolen; so in 1982, another dedication was made, and a new plaque was installed. Alas, it's now also gone. But engraved on the bygone plaque were Sterling's own words about San Francisco:

> *Tho the dark be cold and blind,*
> *Yet her sea fog's touch is kind,*
> *And her mightier caress*
> *Is joy and the pain thereof;*
> *And great is thy tenderness,*
> *O cool, gray city of love!*

Sterling was a serious and prolific poet. In his life he wrote 18 volumes of poetry, 13 of them published by Harry Robertson of San Francisco. Among the more notable were *Wine of Wizardry, The Testimony of the Suns,* and *Lilith*. Sterling met his unfortunate end in 1926 when he was awaiting the arrival of H. L. Mencken, for whom he had made elaborate arrangements in the way of dinners and parties. Mencken, oblivious to Sterling's plans and perhaps even to Sterling himself, decided to stay in Los Angeles a few more days. Sterling was so upset he drank himself into a stupor; when Mencken finally did arrive, Sterling was too drunk to greet him. Sterling also was unable to play his role as master of ceremonies in the festivities in Mencken's honor, so he was promptly replaced. So devastated was Sterling by this social failure that he proceeded to consume a lethal dose of cyanide, right in his room at San Francisco's famed Bohemian Club.

Continue east up the steps and past the tennis courts to Hyde Street. Go left on Hyde Street to Lombard Street.

Before heading down Lombard Street, note that on the northwest corner of Lombard and Hyde is the:

12. **Former home of Robert Louis Stevenson's wife,** 1100 Lombard St., where for years many people believed Stevenson himself resided, although he never did. After Stevenson died, his wife came back to San Francisco and commissioned this house. It's a Willis Polk design.

   Now go right and walk down one of the most famous streets in the world:

13. **Lombard Street.** Known as the "crookedest street in the world" despite the fact that there's a section of Vermont Avenue in the southern part of town that's more crooked, the whimsically winding block of Lombard Street draws thousands of visitors each year (much to the chagrin of neighborhood residents, most of whom would prefer to block off the street to tourists). The angle of the street is so steep that the road has to snake back and forth eight times to make a descent possible. The brick-lined street zigzags around the residences' bright flower gardens, which explode with color during warmer months. This short stretch of Lombard Street is one way, downhill, and is as much fun to walk as it is to drive. Save your film for the bottom where, if you're lucky, you can find a parking space and take a few snapshots of the silly spectacle. You also can walk the block, either up or down, by way of the staircases (without curves) on either side of the street.

   As you descend the final curve on Lombard Street, you'll arrive at the intersection of Lombard and Leavenworth streets. Go left (north) on Leavenworth Street to Chestnut Street, and then turn right and walk down to the:

14. **San Francisco Art Institute,** at 800 Chestnut St. Founded in 1871, it's the oldest art school in the West and has played a central role in the development of contemporary art in the Bay Area. Some people think that the Art Institute's tower is haunted, but that doesn't seem to bother the students who work here. There are three art galleries inside: The Diego Rivera Gallery, located on the

left side of the courtyard, displays student work in addition to the 1931 Rivera mural on the right as you enter; the other two are a photography gallery and a professional gallery, but the most interesting views are those of students working on various projects.

Winding Down Now that you're at the end of the tour, you deserve a snack. Well, lucky for you that within the Art Institute is the beloved **San Francisco Art Institute Café.** One of the best-kept secrets in San Francisco, this cafe offers fresh, affordable fare for Art Institute students as well as in-the-know residents and tourists. The food itself, though tasty, is not actually the draw; it's the view, which extends from Alcatraz Island to Coit Tower and beyond (you might have seen it in the movie *Copycat*—its exterior was the outside of Sigourney Weaver's ridiculously chic apartment). From here, you'll get a bird's-eye view of the San Francisco Bay, as well as a meal of such cafe standards as, sandwiches on fresh-baked bread, soups, salads, and daily specials such as chicken teriyaki with cucumber salad and rice or Indian-style cauliflower with basmati rice; the cafe also serves a wide array of caffeine drinks. A large roof courtyard with cement tables (and the same expansive view) beckons sun-craving diners on sunny days, the perfect spot for a picnic high above the tourist fray. Keep the cafe hours in mind: During the school year, it's open Monday through Thursday from 8am to 5pm, Friday from 8am to 4pm; summer hours are from 9am to 2pm Monday through Friday.

The Majestic Homes of Pacific Heights

Start: Corner of Washington and Laguna streets.

Public Transportation: Bus: 1 to Laguna and Sacramento streets, 12, to TK or 22 (weekdays only) to the corner of Fillmore and Washington streets.

Finish: Corner of Union and Gough streets.

Time: 3 hours, not including shopping stops.

Best Time: Wednesday in the early afternoon, when the Haas-Lilienthal House and the stores are open.

Worst Times: Outside normal shopping hours.

Hills That Could Kill: Octavia Street, between Pacific and Washington streets.

After the cable car line through Pacific Heights was built in 1878, the neighborhood evolved in much the same way as Nob Hill. Vistas were expensive, and only San Francisco's wealthiest could afford to build homes here. Over time, Pacific Heights has become one of San Francisco's most highbrow neighborhoods. As you walk along this tour, you'll find more mansions per block than anywhere else in the city. I've highlighted some of them, mostly those with a story behind them, but there are plenty of other beautiful homes to admire (read: covet) as you walk.

• • • • • • • • • • • • • • • • •

From the corner of Washington and Laguna streets, look for Lafayette Park (which you will visit later) and head toward it, just a few steps along Washington to the:

1. **Mary Phelan Mansion,** at 2150 Washington St. James D. Phelan was mayor of San Francisco from 1894 to 1902, and served as a U.S. senator from 1915 to 1921. He commissioned the building of this Italian Renaissance Revival mansion in 1915 for his sister Mary, because their home had been destroyed in the 1906 earthquake and fire. Neither James nor Mary ever married, and James kept a suite here in his sister's house. Architect Charles Weeks also designed such prominent San Francisco landmarks as the Mark Hopkins hotel and the Chronicle building.

   Go back to Laguna Street and turn right. Continue north, and at the northeast corner of Jackson and Laguna streets you'll see the:

2. **Whittier Mansion,** at 2090 Jackson St., home of the California Historical Society from 1956 to 1991. This understated adobe-colored stone mansion was built in 1896 for William Frank Whittier, a successful paint manufacturer and former director of the utilities company that now is known as Pacific Gas & Electric Company. When architect Edward R. Swain designed this mansion for Whittier, he installed modern technology, including a hydraulic elevator, electric light fixtures, central heat, and steel reinforcement in its brick and Arizona sandstone walls. As a result of Swain's cutting-edge architecture, the mansion withstood the 1906 earthquake and fire.

Pacific Heights

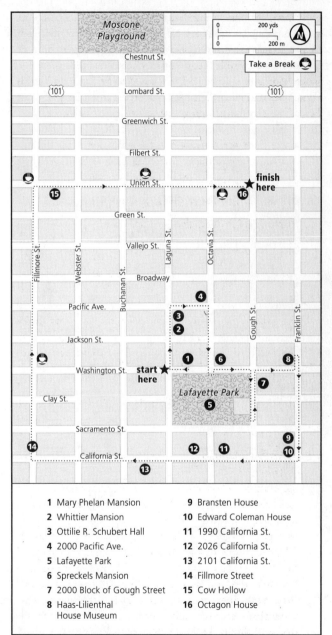

Moscone Playground

Chestnut St.

(101)   Lombard St.   (101)

Greenwich St.

Filbert St.

Union St.   ★ **finish here**

15   **16**

Green St.

Vallejo St.

Broadway

Pacific Ave.   **4**

3
2

Jackson St.

1   **6**   **8**

Washington St.   ★ **start here**

Lafayette Park   **7**

Clay St.   **5**

Sacramento St.

12   **11**   **9**
14   **10**

California St.

13

Fillmore St.
Webster St.
Buchanan St.
Laguna St.
Octavia St.
Gough St.
Franklin St.

Take a Break

0   200 yds
0   200 m

---

1 Mary Phelan Mansion	**9** Bransten House
2 Whittier Mansion	**10** Edward Coleman House
3 Ottilie R. Schubert Hall	**11** 1990 California St.
4 2000 Pacific Ave.	**12** 2026 California St.
5 Lafayette Park	**13** 2101 California St.
6 Spreckels Mansion	**14** Fillmore Street
7 2000 Block of Gough Street	**15** Cow Hollow
8 Haas-Lilienthal House Museum	**16** Octagon House

Unfortunately the mansion is no longer accessible to the public because it's a private residence, but if you were to go inside, you would see walls paneled in every kind of wood imaginable, including birch and mahogany.

Some people believe the house to be haunted by the ghost of William Whittier, but others think it's the ghost of his layabout son, Billy. Billy loved to drink, and because the presence often is detected in the basement where there probably was a wine cellar, I vote for Billy.

Continue past the Whittier Mansion to Pacific Avenue and go right. On the southeast corner, you'll find the:

3. **Ottilie R. Schubert Hall,** at 2099 Pacific Ave. This magnificent Classical Revival house originally was built for John D. Spreckels, Jr., in 1904. Sugar producer Claus (the "Sugar King") Spreckels came to the United States from Hanover, Germany, settling first in New York City and coming later to San Francisco during the gold rush. After he arrived in San Francisco, Spreckels opened a grocery store and then a brewery. From his profits, he started the Bay Sugar Refining Company and became obsessed with sugar, expanding his business to Hawaii. He made Hawaii one of the greatest sugar-producing centers of the world and then sent his son John to Hawaii to oversee business. While there, John Spreckels built a steamer trading line that sailed to the South Seas and Australia.

Continue along Pacific Avenue to:

4. **2000 Pacific Ave.,** which is located at the northwest corner of Pacific Avenue and Octavia Street. This Queen Anne–style home is one of San Francisco's most beautiful Painted Ladies. Note the colonial tower on the right side of the house, and the beautifully detailed frieze around the top. The medallion that stands alone in the center of the facade on the second floor also is worthy of note.

Go right on Octavia Street back up to Washington Street. Directly ahead of you is:

5. **Lafayette Park,** which, in addition to its beauty, has an interesting history that begins with a man named Samuel Holladay. Holladay was one of San Francisco's earliest

residents, and because he couldn't stand the noise and lack of privacy on Montgomery Street, he sought refuge on a nearby hilltop. It wasn't long before he had built himself a house surrounded by a beautiful garden with trees tall enough to keep out the prying stares of passersby. He remained happy on his hill until much later, when the beautiful views of his neighborhood (then called the Western Addition) helped make it one of the most fashionable places to live.

It was then that the city decreed that no person was allowed to live on 2 full city blocks, because that would impede the development of the street grid system. Holladay was told he would have to move, but he refused. Soon he became embroiled in a bitter lawsuit with the city, and Holladay vowed that he wouldn't cut his hair until he won the suit.

The battle continued for many years, and his white hair grew down past his shoulders before a compromise was reached. The city paid Holladay a tidy sum for his land, but instead of cutting the land with a road, the city leveled his house, planted more trees, and added benches, turning the old Holladay place into a public park.

Lafayette Park also is associated with an odd couple— George Davidson, president of the California Academy of Sciences, and James Lick, the quintessential Scrooge. Lick cared nothing for friends, frivolity, or education. The only thing in life he wanted was money—stacks and stacks of it. He arrived in San Francisco in 1847, quickly amassing quite a fortune from real estate. He used some of his fortune to build an elegant hotel, the Lick House, in which he took a room. Being eccentric, however, he didn't choose to live in a beautifully furnished and decorated room; rather, he lived in virtual squalor and often could be seen wandering about town in dirty, ragged clothing.

George Davidson, on the other hand, was a cultured and learned man of moderate means who dedicated his life to teaching. Fate brought them together one evening here in Lafayette Park, Davidson's preferred location for setting up his telescope. Davidson introduced Lick to the stars, and Lick fell in love—probably for the first time in his life. In fact, he was so infatuated with the science of astronomy that he left $700,000 in his will for the building of an observatory on Mount Hamilton. He also left money to the poor and the elderly, and, of course, to the California Academy of Sciences. It was Davidson and the stars that transformed this Scrooge and gave his story a happy ending.

Come back out of the park onto Washington Street and look for the:

6. **Spreckels Mansion,** at 2080 Washington St. Hailed as the "Parthenon of the West," the Spreckels Mansion is one of the grandest homes in San Francisco, taking up an entire block. It once was owned by Adolph Spreckels, another son of the sugar magnate Claus Spreckels (see stop 3 above). Adolph's wife, Alma de Bretteville Spreckels, was an art student at one time, but she also did some modeling for various San Francisco artists. She was the model for the statue of Victory atop the Dewey monument in Union Square, and she also modeled at age 15 for portrait photographer Arnold Genthe. In addition, Alma and Adolph were responsible for the original California Palace of the Legion of Honor in Lincoln Park and its collection of Rodin artwork.

Architect George Applegarth (who later went on to design the Palace of the Legion of Honor) designed the white Utah limestone mansion, which was completed in 1913. The Spreckels mansion has been the set of several movies, including the 1957 film *Pal Joey* (as the nightclub Chez Joey) and the 1969 flick *The Eye of the Cat.* After a period during which the mansion was divided into apartments, romance writer Danielle Steel reportedly dropped a cool $8 million for it in 1990, which doesn't sound like much today for the imposing 55-room estate with paired columns and balconies with scrolled metal balustrades. (Yes, she still owns it.)

Continue east on Washington Street. At the corner of Washington and Gough streets, turn right and walk along the:

7. **2000 block of Gough Street,** which will take you around the other side of Lafayette Park for a look at some

fine Victorian houses, including nos. 2004–2010, built in the Queen Anne style in 1889, and the Eastlake–Queen Anne home just a few doors down at no. 2000. It was built in 1889.

Turn around and go back along Gough Street to Washington. Turn right on Washington and walk to Franklin Street, and then turn left on Franklin, where you'll find the:

8. **Haas-Lilienthal House Museum,** at 2007 Franklin St., also the headquarters for San Francisco Architectural Heritage.

You definitely should make time to visit this house, not only because it is one of the city's most spectacular Queen Anne–style Victorians, but because it's furnished with period pieces and you'll get a rare glimpse at the history of an old San Francisco family. Alice Haas-Lilienthal, daughter of the original owners of the house, lived here from 1886 to 1972 and was able to preserve the house and its contents in spite of the ups and downs of the neighborhood. Two years after Alice's death, her family donated the house to the foundation, which offers tours every half-hour on Wednesday and Saturday from noon to 3pm and Sunday from 11am to 4pm. Arrive 15 minutes prior to the tour you intend to take. (Sorry, you can't tour solo.) Admission for the tour is $8 for adults and $5 for seniors and children.

When you exit the house, turn south onto Franklin, continuing past Washington Street to the:

9. **Bransten House,** at 1735 Franklin St. Built in 1904, this Georgian Revival house was a wedding gift of the Haas family to their daughter Florine and her new husband, Edward Bransten, a coffee magnate. After her husband died in 1948, Florine Haas Bransten lived here for nearly 30 years—and presumably hosted her sister Alice (see stop 8), who lived only 3 blocks away, from time to time.

Continue along to the:

10. **Edward Coleman House,** at 1701 Franklin St. (on the corner of California St.). Built in 1895, this Queen

Anne–style gem once served as a boarding house, and was in decent shape when a law firm purchased it and did a full restoration in 1975. Note the wonderful round corner tower and the enormous bay windows.

Turn right on California Street and walk until you reach:

11. **1990 California St.,** the former home of Dominga de Goni, mother-in-law of author Gertrude Atherton. After Dominga's husband died in 1880, she moved from her country home into this sprawling mansion and was joined by her son, George, and her daughter-in-law, Gertrude.

Novelist Gertrude Atherton married into this well-to-do family almost by accident. George proposed to her five times before she consented, and after they were married, she was miserable; she described him as practically illiterate, boring, and nagging, and went so far as to say, "The worst trial I had yet been called upon to endure was having a husband continually on my hands." (For more information on Gertrude Atherton's literary pursuits, see stop 13.)

George's mother, it seems, agreed wholeheartedly, and between Gertrude's brush-offs and his mother's insults, George was a rather unhappy man. In an effort to get away from both of them, he decided to take a trip to Chile. He was out to sea for only a couple of days when his kidney ruptured and he died. George's cousin, who was accompanying him, placed his body in a barrel of rum and sent it back to San Francisco.

Gertrude and Dominga Atherton soon began to feel a ghostly presence in the house. Naturally they assumed it was George (more likely it was guilt), and not long after his death, they moved out. Since then, other tenants have noticed strange goings-on in the house, and one or two have even seen an apparition hanging about. A séance revealed four presences (Gertrude, George, Dominga, and a woman who once ran a boarding house here).

Continue along California Street to:

12. **2026 California St.** Located between Octavia and Laguna streets, this Italianate home with its rather blatant

blue, bronze, and white color scheme is a stately addition to this block. Note the Egyptian head above the doorway—it is reflected in the interior in an Egyptian mural above the fireplace.

Continue on to:

13. **2101 California St.,** on your left. Gertrude Atherton had an apartment here beginning in 1929, in which (among other places) she held literary functions and salons until she was well into her 80s. A former member of the literary group Les Jeunes, and one of America's first true feminists, Atherton wrote such novels as *The Doomswoman* (1892) and *Black Oxen* (1923), the latter a bestseller. She was one of San Francisco's most important writers, and before her death in 1948, she published one of her most interesting books, *My San Francisco,* which chronicles the history of some of San Francisco's most famous and infamous residents.

Continue on California Street, past Buchanan and Webster streets, and turn right onto:

14. **Fillmore Street,** which has been in transformation due to the recent economic downturn. Currently it's flooded with women's boutiques, bath and beauty shops, and cafes and restaurants, including a few worthy stops. First, indulge yourself with a high-calorie treat at **Bittersweet,** 2123 Fillmore St., a new chocolate cafe featuring 120 chocolate bars from around the world, chocolate pastries, confections, and drinks. Next door there's owner/author/chef Carlo Middione's **Vivande Porta Via** (at no. 2125), which has a mouthwatering assortment of Italian gourmet groceries, plus a great little Italian trattoria that serves excellent southern Italian fare such as pasta Carbonara Romano or pasta with besaola (thinly sliced cured beef) and arugula. It borders on expensive, so if you're on a budget and thinking about lunch, try one of the other, less-expensive places along Fillmore Street that I recommend later. But if you feel like splurging and you can find an empty table or counter space, by all means do.

A bit farther on is a well-stocked bookstore called **Browser Books** (at no. 2195).

Take a Break   Several different eateries occupy this stretch of Fillmore Street (in addition to Vivande Porta Via), making them convenient stops for lunch or a snack. One that makes it worth backtracking south down Fillmore is **Chez Nous** (at 1911 Fillmore St. between Pine and Bush sts.), which serves delicate, fresh, unfussy, French-influenced salads, soups, and entrees such as gnocchi or grilled lamb loin chops.

Continue up (north) Fillmore Street to Broadway where you should pause to revel in the incredible view of the water beyond the rooftops. Then follow Fillmore all the way to Union Street. At the intersection of Fillmore and Union streets, you'll be in the heart of:

15. **Cow Hollow,** so named because of the 30 dairy farms that were here in 1861. Also located in this area was a small pond known as Washerwoman's Lagoon, the city's primitive laundromat. However, in the latter part of the 19th century, pollution from the slaughterhouses, tanneries, and meatpacking factories forced the city to close the dairies. Farms were never allowed in the city again, and the polluted lagoon was filled in with sand.

Since the 1950s, around the time the Beat poets held their readings at the Six Gallery, Union Street has evolved into a shopper's delight, and if you turn right on Union Street from the corner of Fillmore Street, you'll find 7 blocks of boutiques, specialty shops, bookstores, and art galleries. Many of them are housed in some fine old Victorian homes. Before you get to the intersection of Buchanan Street, you'll see no. 2040 on your left. Although it's now a minicomplex of shops and galleries, it was one of the original Cow Hollow Victorian farmhouses. Also on this block you'll see Betelnut, a chic "contemporary Asian" restaurant. Located at 2030 Union St., it's a glamorous (and expensive) place to order salt-and-pepper whole gulf prawns, pots stickers, chicken satay, and green tea cocktails, and watch the young and beautiful locals schmooze at the bar. (More on why you might want to eat here later.)

As you walk east along Union Street, keep an eye out for the last stop on the tour, the:

16. **Octagon House,** at the corner of Union and Gough streets (2645 Gough). It was built in 1861, and now is a museum and home to the National Society of Colonial Dames of America. This unusual, eight-sided, cupola-topped house was built at a time when it was rumored that octagonal spaces made for a healthier existence, and although it makes for interesting architecture, there was never any proof that this claim was true. The architectural features, however, are extraordinary, and from the second floor it is possible to look up into the cupola, which is illuminated at night.

   If you're here on a day when the house is open—on the second Sunday and second and fourth Thursdays of every month (except Jan, when it's closed) between noon and 3pm—you should go inside because it is interesting to see how the space has been divided up. Bedrooms and major living spaces are square, and the leftover triangular spaces serve as bathrooms and closets. Also inside you'll find Early American furniture, portraits, silver, pewter, looking glasses, and English and Chinese ceramics. The museum also houses some historic documents, including signatures of 54 of the 56 signers of the Declaration of Independence.

   Winding Down   If all this walking has worked up your appetite, you're in luck, because two fine restaurants—both open for lunch and dinner—are right on Union Street. You can either return to **Betelnut** for an upscale Asian experience (© **415/929-8855**) or go super-casual Italian at **Pane e Vino** at 1715 Union St. between Gough and Octavia streets (© **415/346-2111**), right next to the Octagon house.

   Why these two spots?
   Although San Francisco is teeming with Chinese restaurants, few offer such a posh, fashionable dining environment as Betelnut. As the menu explains, the restaurant is themed after "Pejui Wu," a traditional Asian beer house offering local brews and savory dishes. But with the bamboo paneling, red Formica countertops, and low-hanging lamps, the place feels less like an authentic harbor restaurant and more like a set from the Madonna

movie *Shanghai Surprise.* Still, the atmosphere is en vogue, with dimly lit booths, ringside seating overlooking the bustling stir-fry chefs, sidewalk tables (weather permitting), and body-to-body flirting at the cramped but festive bar. If nothing else, come for the heavenly signature dessert: a mouthwatering tapioca pudding with sweet red adzuki beans.

As for **Pane e Vino,** a down-home Italian trattoria, the food is nothing fancy, just classic Italian fare in a friendly, casual environment. The prices are reasonable, and the mostly Italian-accented staff is always smooth and efficient under pressure. Most important, the pastas, such as their flavorful *pennette alla boscaiola* with porcini mushrooms and pancetta in a tomato cream sauce, are quite nice. Top dessert picks are any of the Italian ice creams, the crème caramel, and (but of course) the creamy tiramisu. Though it's not a "destination restaurant," it certainly does the trick, especially if you don't want any pomp with your pasta.

If you wish to return to the start of this tour, you have two options, neither of which is particularly speedy. You can either walk up Gough Street for 6 blocks and turn right on Washington Street to Lafayette Park (a real workout), or catch the no. 22 bus at Union and Steiner streets, get off at Fillmore and Washington streets, and walk 3 blocks east on Washington Street to Lafayette Park.

Better yet, catch either the no. 41 or 45 bus heading due east on Union Street, get off at Columbus Avenue, and continue your exploration of San Francisco with a tour of North Beach.

South of Market: A Civilized Afternoon of Arts & Leisure

Start: Mission Street, between Fourth and Fifth streets.

Public Transportation: Bus: 15, 30, or 45; Muni Metro: J, K, L, or M to Montgomery Station.

Finish: New Montgomery and Market streets.

Time: Half an hour to 5 hours, depending on how many museums you visit.

Best Times: Tuesday and Thursday through Saturday from 11am to 5pm.

Worst Times: Monday, when many of the museums are closed; Wednesday, when the Museum of Modern Art is closed; Sunday; nighttime.

Hills That Could Kill: None.

Several years ago, I noted that South of Market was in the middle of its second coming. Today, it's straight-up booming. Its first coming, though not as elaborate, was after the 1849 gold rush, when the rich moved out of the city's center (now Chinatown) and headed for what today would be considered the suburbs. Sure, South of Market was only a few blocks south, but at the time it was nothing but sunny, pristine hillside a decent walk or a pleasant carriage ride away.

Today, little evidence remains that SoMa was a rich enclave, but its new identity is equally enticing. With almost no space left to build in San Francisco, in recent years the city government, residents, merchants, museums, and, for a brief instant, the dot.com industry flocked to this industrial area for redevelopment and expansion. The result? The blocks beyond Market, just south of Union Square, have become a mecca of art galleries, restaurants, loft and condo residences, and even nightlife and national league baseball.

This tour will give you a peek into varied aspects of SoMa: You'll see several museums, visit a few historical areas, check out ghostly imprints of the dot.com industry, and, inevitably, encounter some of the city's less attractive streets. Before you go, it's a good idea to first read over the chapter and decide which museums you'd like to visit; almost all of them have admission fees and will take up a good portion of time as well as money.

• • • • • • • • • • • • • • • •

Because you're most likely coming from the Union Square area, we'll start you off at the closest attraction, which also is near the Mission and Fifth Street parking garage (the most convenient in the area). Just 1 major block south of

South of Market

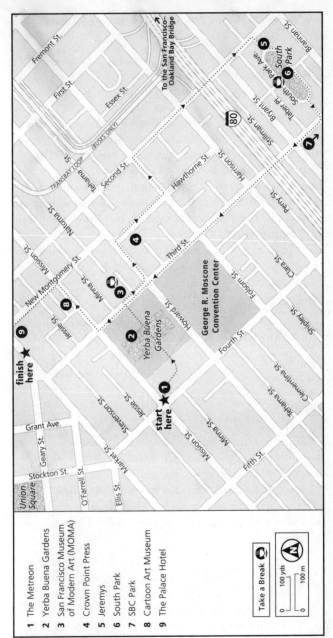

Take a Break 🔵

0 ——— 100 yds
0 ——— 100 m

1 The Metreon
2 Yerba Buena Gardens
3 San Francisco Museum of Modern Art (MOMA)
4 Crown Point Press
5 Jeremys
6 South Park
7 SBC Park
8 Cartoon Art Museum
9 The Palace Hotel

Market on Mission Street at the corner of Fourth Street is our first stop:

1. **The Metreon,** Sony's entertainment center (© **415/ 369-6000**). It's a 350,000-square-foot complex packed with innovative and fun ways to help you part with your money. Along with a massive multiplex movie theater and the largest IMAX theater in North America are a number of restaurants and an arcade complete with a high-tech version of bowling. Even the shops, which include Digital Solutions and a Sony store, are designed to offer entertainment value. You might want to note the lobby's food court; it features a number of annexes to full-fledged San Francisco restaurants, and could be considered one of the best in fast food.

   Once you've had enough of the Metreon, head out the door farthest from the one you entered. You'll be in the midst of:

2. **Yerba Buena Gardens,** where you'll find a spectacular cross-culture of San Franciscans. Old Chinese couples, tourists, sunbathers (weather permitting), art admirers, lunching professionals—they all come here to enjoy the one grassy expanse offering respite from the surrounding concrete desert.

   Eventually, all paths here lead to the mixed-media water sculpture tribute to Martin Luther King, Jr. The moving and misty memorial includes the socially and artistically relevant statement:

   > *No. No, we are not satisfied, and we will not*
   > *be satisfied until justice rolls down like water*
   > *and righteousness like a mighty stream.*
   > *—Martin Luther King, Jr.*
   > *Washington, D.C., 1963*

   Children, who are particularly taken with the memorial's rushing waterfalls and damp walkway, might not understand the significance of the powerful piece, but they love it just the same.

   The building situated on the eastern outskirts of the gardens is home to **Yerba Buena Center for the Arts**

(© **415/978-2787;** www.ybca.org), which features cutting-edge visual arts, performing arts, and film and video
programs. Check out their schedule to see if it's worth a
detour during opening hours, which are noon to 5pm
Sunday, Tuesday, and Wednesday and noon to 8pm
Thursday through Saturday.

After you've finished exploring, follow the path that
cuts through the park, passing the memorial on the right,
and leads to Third Street. Cross Third to get to the
entrance of the:

3. **San Francisco Museum of Modern Art** (MOMA;
   © **415/357-4000;** www.sfmoma.org). Some argue that
   the best thing about this museum—which was built by
   Swiss architect Mario Botta in association with Hellmuth,
   Obata, and Kassabaum to replace its previous unworthy
   Civic Center location—is the building itself. Considering
   the untraditional, somewhat cramped exhibition spaces,
   the topic is a worthy debate. Nonetheless, the city's $62-
   million modern art museum is one hot attraction and
   worth its admission price. The museum's collection consists of more than 15,000 works (with a small portion on
   display at any given time), including close to 5,000 paintings and sculptures by such artists as Henri Matisse,
   Jackson Pollock, Willem de Kooning, Diego Rivera,
   Georgia O'Keeffe, Paul Klee, and the Fauvists. MOMA
   also has an exceptional collection of Richard Diebenkorn's
   paintings. Because MOMA was one of the first museums
   to recognize photography as a major art form, its collection includes more than 9,000 photographs by such mas-
   ters as Ansel Adams, Alfred Stieglitz, Edward Weston, and
   Henri Cartier-Bresson. The museum is open Friday
   through Tuesday from 11am to 5:45pm and Thursday
   from 11am to 8:45pm. It's closed on Wednesday, is free
   the first Tuesday of each month, and has extended summer hours, opening at 10am Tuesday through Sunday
   from Memorial Day through Labor Day. *Tip:* Tickets are
   half price on Thursday from 6 to 8:45pm. Admission is
   $13 for adults, $8 for seniors (62+), and $7 for students
   with ID.

Whether you choose to visit the museum or not, a must-stop is MOMA's adjoining MuseumStore (as you exit the building, it's on your immediate right at 151 Third St.), which carries a wonderful array of architectural gifts, books, and trinkets, as well as the most creative and tasteful tourist mementos in town.

Yet another reason to spend more time and money at MOMA is the ideal place to:

☕ **Take a Break** **Caffè Museo,** which you couldn't help but see as you approached the museum and will again find if you take a left when exiting the MuseumStore, is just south of the museum entrance at 151 Third St. This cafe sets the standard for museum food, with flavorful and fresh soups, sandwiches, and salads that are as respectable as those served in many local restaurants. The Italian-inspired fare includes tasty *panini,* lasagna, and homemade baked goods, almost all of which cost around $9 to $11. You must, of course, have a coffee drink as well—you're in the heart of cafe culture.

On sunny days, the outside aluminum seating is preferable, allowing street-side views of Third Street and Yerba Buena bustle. However, inside is a far better option when the city's fickle weather acts up.

Once you've lounged long enough, exit the cafe, turn left, and head toward the corner of Howard and Third. (Note that you're standing in front of the entrance of the W Hotel. Should you want a lively cocktail scene come sundown, head to the upstairs bar here for a flashy young crowd toting martinis and crowding into seating nooks.) Cross Howard and head east until you come upon an unobtrusive alley called Hawthorne Street on your right. Turn right onto it, and you'll instantly come to 20 Hawthorne, home of:

4. **Crown Point Press** (℅ 415/974-6273; www.crown point.com). Established in 1962, this printmaking studio and gallery is world renowned for introducing, promoting, and making accessible the etching medium to some of the world's finest artists. Here, artists, many of whom

have never before attempted the printed art form, come by invitation to explore the medium, make art, and contribute to what is now one of the leading fine-art print publishers in America.

As you take the elevator up to the second floor gallery, don't expect huge exhibit halls—it's an airy establishment, which shows monthly exhibits of prints and lots of books. You may call ahead for a tour of the studio. Crown Point is open Tuesday through Saturday from 10am to 6pm.

Exit Crown Point and turn right. (Take a peek inside Hawthorne Lane next door if you want to know where to have a wonderfully refined lunch or dinner while you're in the 'hood.) At the end of the block, turn left onto Folsom. When you reach Second Street, turn right and follow it south for several blocks. Unfortunately, there's not a lot to look at on the way, other than empty retail spaces once filled to the rafters with dot.commers. But just when you think I've sent you into a never-ending concrete nightmare, you can consider stopping at:

5. **Jeremys,** at 2 South Park (the entrance is on Second), for a little retail therapy. This beautiful store offers top designer fashions, from shoes to suits and gowns, at rock-bottom prices. You won't find any cheap knockoffs here, just entirely fashionable clothes and accessories for far less than you'll pay elsewhere.

Exit Jeremys and turn right onto:

6. **South Park,** one of SoMa's sweetest attributes, and previously famous as the heart of the daily dot.com caffeine and lunching scene, today's South Park is amazingly quiet and quaint. During the dot.com heyday, this residential enclave was one of the hottest spots in town. However, even then, few who frequented the area knew exactly why this obvious diversion from surrounding architecture and overall neighborhood planning exists.

A little research would inform them that shortly after the 1849 gold rush, the wealthy moved their money out of established San Francisco to this sunny retreat just south of downtown. Take a good look at the area and imagine it: London Regency–style town houses surrounding the grassy common, horse-drawn carriages circling the street, and, because there were few other buildings in the area, lovely views. Today the gritty and looming industrial SoMa streets do a good job of ruining the fantasy. But this little circular street does have a few stop-worthy shops as well as a casual, affordable lunchtime respite, which you will find at 102 South Park, the perfect place to:

☕ **Take a Break** At **Caffe Centro** you'll find an excellent—and cheap—place to buy a bit of ambience along with a revitalizing mocha. Its limited kitchen and ultracasual cafe style will keep this spot from ever becoming a destination, but its simple and cozy space, too-quaint sidewalk seating, and view of the common make it the perfect place to catch a few rays, read the paper, and simply exist. The only reminder that you're in a big city is the remaining hip, high-tech-industry professionals who straggle in for a dose of high-octane java and a lunch of flavorful bread salad, sandwiches, and a breakfast of pastries, fruit, granola, and poached eggs. Don't show up hungry on a Sunday: The place is closed.

Time for one more diversion before heading back toward Union Square. Exit the west side of South Park (opposite the side from which you entered) and take a left onto Third Street. Follow Third for 2½ blocks and you'll be standing in front of:

7. **SBC Park.** Previously Pacific Bell Park and destined to be renamed after a slew of future sponsors, the stunning $319-million home of the San Francisco Giants (www.sfgiants.com) is drop-dead gorgeous with its unobstructed bay vistas, complete with bobbing boats beyond the outfield. Even those who don't care for spectator sports are making the pilgrimage. Notice the Willie Mays statue and inlaid brick in the shape of a baseball in front of the restaurant **Acme Chophouse** (open Tues–Sun for dinner only). If you want to root for the home team (or otherwise), you can call **BASS Ticketmaster** at ☎ **510/ 762-2277.**

Now comes the part where you get a glimpse of the less attractive San Francisco. From here, unfortunately, it's a bit of an ugly, concrete-and-warehouse walk back. Head back down Third Street toward downtown and follow it until you reach the Museum of Modern Art area.

For two last hurrahs, you might want to continue on Third to Mission Street, and turn right on Mission. Halfway down the block, at 655 Mission, you'll encounter the:

8. **Cartoon Art Museum** (*©* 415/CARTOON; www. cartoonart.org). It's a whimsical way to wind down the tour, with 6,000 works in their permanent collection and a historical perspective of cartoon arts, underground comics, rotating exhibits, such as a recent one showcasing "Garfield: Meow and Then." The admission isn't cheap (adults $6, students and seniors $4, kids 6–12 $2, free for children under 6), but if you're into cartoon art, it's definitely worth your while. Even if you don't cruise the gallery, you can check out the quirky gift shop. *Note:* The museum is open Tuesday through Sunday from 11am to 5pm and is closed on Monday; the first Tuesday of the month is "pay what you wish day."

Once you've had your fill, turn right onto Mission as you exit the building and take another left onto New Montgomery. Just before Market Street, you'll get a blast from the past with a visit to:

9. **The Palace Hotel.** This is the location of the original Palace Hotel, which, upon its completion in 1875, was the largest hotel in the United States. At a $5-million construction cost, it also was the most expensive. The original structure (which burned after the 1906 quake) was seven solid stories of luxury, with 800 rooms, and a guest list that included Prince Louis Napoleon Bonaparte, Oscar Wilde, and Theodore Roosevelt. From the rubble of 1906 came the hotel's replacement, another Palace built in 1909, with an equally distinguished clientele that included Presidents Taft, McKinley, Wilson, and Harding and Hawaii's King David Kalakaua.

Take a walk through the lobby. Even countless renovations haven't entirely squelched the hotel's majestic, old-world feel. As spectacular as the old regal lobby is the

Garden Court, a San Francisco landmark that's been restored to its original 1909 grandeur. Take a peek into the Garden Court, if only to look at the massive Italian-marble Ionic columns, enormous chandeliers, and the 80,000-pane stained-glass ceiling.

You also might want to duck into the Pied Piper Bar to check out its $5-million Maxfield Parrish mural.

Upon leaving the hotel, if you turn left, you'll find yourself on Market Street, where you can catch any number of public buses or, if you've got the stamina, head a few blocks northwest to embark on the Union Square tour.

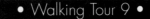

The Culture & Color of the Mission District

Start: Corner of 24th and Mission streets.

Public Transportation: Bus: 14, 14L, 26, 48, 49, or 67; BART: 24th/Mission.

Finish: 16th and Dolores streets.

Time: 3 to 4 hours, not including shopping time.

Best Times: Monday through Saturday from 9am to 5pm.

Worst Times: Before 9am or after 5pm when shops are closed, and after dusk when the area becomes a bit sketchy.

Hills That Could Kill: None.

In 1776, almost 75 years before the city took shape, the Spanish arrived in what would become the Mission neighborhood. Although these official first foreigners left their mark in the form of the adobe Mission Dolores, they abandoned the area by the 1800s.

Then, at the beginning of the 19th century, a 40-foot-wide road similar to a boardwalk was laid here. The Mission District quickly filled with gambling houses, saloons, and brothels, as well as farmhouses and private homes. Its population grew rapidly, and people of many different ethnic groups, including Germans, Italians, Americans, and Irish, settled in.

Ultimately, the city's Latin community concentrated in the Mission and over time became its primary populace. The neighborhood is still multiethnic; American Indians, Asians, Filipinos, a small community of Irish, and most recently a melting pot of young, alternative artistic types reside in relative harmony. (As one of the last affordable areas to live in town, the Mission also is a bit rougher than some of the other neighborhoods you've visited on these tours.) It also holds some of the city's greatest treasures, including a huge number of outdoor murals; the city's oldest standing structure; handsome Victorian homes; and a wealth of cultural sites, restaurants, and shops.

This tour will take you through one of the most exotic neighborhoods in San Francisco. You will walk along the ethnic shopping streets and through Balmy Alley and its mural mania, savor some of the city's finest Mexican food, and finally end up at the city's oldest building, historic Mission Dolores.

If you're feeling lazy after exploring the 24th Street area, we recommend you either jump in your car or take the bus from Mission Street to Mission Dolores Park, where you can continue the rest of the tour. The blocks leading there are long and not very scenic.

• • • • • • • • • • • • • • • •

A word of warning: If you bring your car down here, practice caution as you would in any metropolitan city. Make sure any valuables are not visible from outside of the car. That said, begin at the busiest corner in the Mission District:

1. **24th and Mission.** No matter what time of day or year, there's always something going on here. At least one or

Mission District

1 24th and Mission
2 24th Street
3 *Carnaval*
4 Discolandia
5 Casa Lucas Market
6 La Palma Mexica-tessen
7 Galeria de la Raza
8 Dominguez Bakery
9 Balmy Alley
10 Garfield Square
11 Mission Cultural Center
12 23rd Street
13 Mission Playground
14 Mission Dolores Park
15 Mission Dolores
16 Basilica of San Francisco

two soapbox prophets preach to passersby in Spanish. Another righteous soul might be handing out pamphlets regarding the human injustices suffered by immigrant laborers. And hordes of people scurry to and from the Mission Street BART station, whose underground system transports residents in and out of the area. The abundant, somewhat overwhelming, eye candy alone is worth the trip, but if you walk to the northeast corner of Mission and 24th, behind the row of trees you will notice a striking mural. It's most visible when the sycamores lose their leaves, but regardless, if you stand close enough you will see *BART,* which was painted in acrylic by muralists Michael Rios, Anthony Machado, and Richard Montez in 1975. It's not difficult to absorb the slightly disturbing undertones of the work; androgynous figures support the rails upon which the BART train rides, bending beneath its weight. The train itself, with its angular lead car, appears as a menacing snake. Masses of the same genderless figures stand behind those who hold the tracks.

Follow the line of the depicted BART train, and you'll see the entrance to the BART station.

If your goal is to see all the Mission District murals, start counting; you've got 1 down, around 200 to go. We'll be passing many, but not even close to all of them.

From here, turn your attention to:

2. **24th Street,** the heart of the Latino shopping district. Beginning here and running east for several blocks are wall-to-wall specialty shops—Latino bakeries, bookstores, and grocery stores—as well as what amounts to one of the most exotically foreign walks in town (second only to Chinatown).

Follow 24th Street east, toward the bay, walk two short blocks and stop at the corner of South Van Ness. On the right side of the street, you can't miss:

3. **Carnaval,** another mural, painted in 1983 in oil enamel by muralists Daniel Galvez, Dan Fontes, and others; the artists have cleverly turned this otherwise boring, blank facade and block into a row of beautiful Painted Ladies.

To add to the festive feeling created by the jazzy colors used to dress up the faux Victorian homes, the artists added the dancers, the drummer, and the crowd gathered "between" the buildings on the left; it's a depiction of the wild Latin American celebration that takes place in the community each year over Memorial Day weekend.

Cross 24th Street to get to the left side of the street and continue east. Cross Folsom and Harrison streets, and in the middle of the block, at 2964 24th, you will hear music playing from within:

4. **Discolandia,** the neighborhood's infamous CD and record store. A visit here can feel like you're walking into the middle of a family gathering. Often there's a small crowd chatting around the sales counter, while others shuffle through the vast collection of Latino music, which ranges from Peruvian to Puerto Rican.

Turn left out the door, again walking along the left side of 24th. Cross Alabama Street, and you will quickly come to no. 2934, the building housing:

5. **Casa Lucas Market.** You probably won't want to lug exotic groceries around on your tour, but to get an idea of the unique ingredients used in everyday Latin American cooking, check out this wonderful neighborhood shop. Walk past the cornucopia of fruit stacked at the sidewalk stand and wind your way through the aisles. In the vegetable department, you'll find a robust selection of fresh chiles and yuccas. In the back of the store, bins are filled with dried beans, chiles, and grains, and along the side wall at the very back of the store hang spices you've probably never heard of, let alone can pronounce. Notice the piñatas hanging over the checkout counters. Here, too, you will find colorful candies and unidentifiable desserts.

On your way out, note the mural across the street, which pictures a vibrant, flourishing farming village. Don't bother crossing the street; you're going to hit that side of the street on the way back to Mission Street.

Follow 24th Street farther and cross Florida Street. At 2884 24th St., you'll want to stop at the:

6. **La Palma Mexica-tessen.** It looks like another little traditional Mexican market, and it is. But in-the-know locals come here for the city's only freshly handmade tortillas. Check it out for yourself: Look beyond the counter, and you'll see women mixing ingredients and patiently patting down doughy discs while recorded ranchero ballads help them keep pace. You'll undoubtedly be intrigued by the "pupusas," a Salvadorean version of calzone, behind glass at the snack counter. Go ahead and snack lightly. The tacos, flautas, freshly made salsa—everything's good and under $7. Do save room, however: One of the city's best Mexican meals is still to come. Locals also come here for *masa,* a ground cornmeal used in Mexican baking and cooking.

Upon exiting the store, turn left and go to the corner of 24th and Bryant. Cross 24th Street, and on the southwest corner you'll be standing in front of:

7. **Galeria de la Raza,** established in 1970 to promote public knowledge and appreciation of Chicano and Latino art and the indigenous cultures from which they arise. Today, this small gallery receives worldwide recognition for its captivating and culturally significant exhibitions, which change every 6 to 8 weeks.

To help support itself, in 1976, Galeria de la Raza opened the adjoining gift shop:

Studio 24, 2857 24th St. Good luck escaping this fun little Latin American import shop without buying something. From the romantically luminous "perpetually burning" candles to papier-mâché dolls, calendars, and silver jewelry, everything here is artistic and affordable. The in-store gallery changes monthly.

Walk just a block farther and you'll stumble upon **Roosevelt Tamale Parlor** at 2817 24th St. It's one of the oldest and cheapest around. At 2801 24th St., you'll find **St. Francis Fountain & Candy Store,** which was established in 1918 and is still beloved for its homemade ice cream and old-fashioned creamery vibe.

Now you're going to head back toward Mission Street. Following the south side of 24th Street, walk west, cross

Florida Street, cross Alabama, and you'll be standing in front of:

8. **Dominguez Bakery,** 2951 24th St. If you're interested in sampling Mexican pastries, go to the counter of this family-owned shop, which has been in business since 1965. Grab a tray and a pair of tongs, and head to the back, where you can snatch up *pan dulce* (sweet bread) galore. *Pan huevo* (egg bread), *elotes* (corn-shaped sweet bread), churros (weekends only), pumpkin turnovers, *sevillanas* (Mexican wedding cookies): you name it—if you can—they've got it. Don't stuff yourself, though. You'll be visiting one of the city's most extraordinary taco and burrito restaurants within the hour.

That's enough with the edible temptations. Now ready yourself for a feast for the eyes. Again, go west on 24th Street. Cross Harrison Street, and take a left at the next alley. You've found:

9. **Balmy Alley,** which must surely boast the largest number of murals per square foot in the world.

The mural project in Balmy Alley began unofficially in the late 1970s, but it wasn't until the early 1980s that a group calling itself PLACA (*placa* is a word for a graffiti artist's tag name) came together to paint as many murals as possible on this little street.

In 1984, they began the project (privately funded by people who lived and worked in the Mission District) that monopolized their free time—they worked free of charge—and resulted in 28 new murals. They dedicated the murals with a parade and celebration down Balmy Alley. (But, of course, this community has a parade and celebration in honor of every new mural.) The murals were restored in 1990.

Follow Balmy Alley to 25th Street and you'll be faced with:

10. **Garfield Square.** Here you'll find several murals, two of which are on the community building that houses the public swimming pool. On the 26th Street side is *The Primal Sea,* which was painted by the local mural group

Precita Eyes in 1980. On the Harrison side is a mural painted by Domingo Rivera in 1973, which has an Aztec and Mayan theme.

Get your fill of the square and then exit on 25th Street. Head right (west) until you reach Mission Street. Take a right on Mission and until you arrive at a clean and straightforward eatery (yes, the one we've been preparing you for) called:

Take a Break **La Taqueria,** 2889 Mission St., between 24th and 25th streets. This is one of San Franciscans' favorite Mexican haunts. La Taqueria is especially known for its tacos, which come in the usual, excellent variations plus hard-core favorites: beef head and beef tongue. Also worthy are the burritos. For the full effect, order a Mexican fruit drink, too, and then pull up a leather crosshatched bench and enjoy one of the city's worst-kept secrets.

There's always room for dessert, so take a right out of La Taqueria, and on your right you'll instantly come across **Dianda's,** at 2883 Mission St. It might seem out of place, but this excellent Italian bakery has been in the neighborhood since 1969. Indulge in at least one super-sinful treat: cake, cookies, pastries, panettone, whatever. Everything here comes highly recommended.

Double back to the corner of 25th and Mission. Cross Mission, take a right, and halfway down the block you'll find the:

11. **Mission Cultural Center,** 2826 Mission St., an excellent community center that provides the neighborhood with an extensive array of dance, art, karate, and other classes. Appropriately, the exterior of the Cultural Center is decorated with a mural that depicts Native American Mexicans. Carlos Loarca, who collaborated with Manuel Villamor and Betsie Miller-Kusz in the painting of the exterior of this building, was one of the first muralists to paint in the Mission. He also taught classes here in the 1970s.

Walk inside, and you'll get the feeling there's nothing to see here. But if you take the stairs to the right of the lobby, they'll lead you to the second-floor art gallery, which exhibits local works that change monthly. The room gets especially festive around the end of October when the *Dia de los Muertos* (Day of the Dead) celebration is honored with altars and traditional decorations displayed throughout the room.

Along with the Day of the Dead celebration, the Mission Cultural Center plays a large role in other community activities and organizes a variety of events for the residents of this neighborhood.

As you exit the Cultural Center, go left on Mission. Cross 24th Street, and when you get to 23rd Street, cross to the northeast side of Mission Street. You're making a quick detour onto:

12. **23rd Street,** where you'll almost immediately find two more murals. One simply consists of various types of greenery, whereas the other, outside Casa Grande, a ceramics and tile store, is worth spending some time looking at because each face is distinct and culturally different.

Now return to Mission Street and continue west to Valencia Street. Cross the street, go right on Valencia, and follow it for several blocks until you reach 19th Street. Make a quick left to arrive at the:

13. **Mission Playground,** where you'll find another stunning mural, *The New World Tree,* painted in 1987 by Juana Alicia, Susan Cervantes, and Raul Martinez.

This mural is particularly pleasing not only because the blues and greens create a sense of calm for the viewer, but also because they reflect the colors in the sky, grass, trees, and presumably the pool, which lies behind these beautiful walls.

The branches of the tree hold a man and boy on one side, a woman and girl on the other. The man and woman are joined together at the top by the baby, who radiates orange light like the sun. All human elements in the painting are of different cultures, and the mural seems to present a new Eden, one with other human figures sitting under trees (one man has his hand in the river), forest animals, and a sailing ship.

The mural extends around the side of the building, so do go around and take a look.

Exit the north end of the Mission Playground onto 19th Street. Go left on 19th Street and follow it to Dolores Street. You'll be directly in front of:

14. **Mission Dolores Park,** which consisted of two Jewish cemeteries when the land was purchased in 1861. Later, when the cemeteries hampered the city's expansion, the remains of most people buried here (and other cemeteries around the city) were exhumed and moved to new cemeteries well outside the boundaries of San Francisco proper. Today this park, which was laid out in 1905, is the biggest in the Mission District.

At the corner of 19th and Dolores streets is a replica of Mexico's Liberty Bell, which was donated in 1962. On the opposite side of the park, on the corner of Church and 20th streets (diagonally across the park from where you stand now), you can enjoy a panoramic view of the city.

After you've absorbed the view, go back to 19th and Dolores streets and continue up (going left out of the park) to 18th Street, where you'll see two more murals.

Then walk up Dolores Street to:

15. **Mission Dolores,** at 16th and Dolores streets. Officially called Mission San Francisco de Assisi, this was the sixth of 21 California missions established by Father Junípero Serra. The first group of explorers arrived here on June 27, 1776, and the first service was held by Father Francisco Palou 2 days later under a tent. Palou also was responsible for the design of the mission you see today.

Building began on this adobe structure in 1782, and was completed in 1791. It has survived all the earthquakes and fires that have plagued the city over the years and is the oldest building standing in the city of San Francisco today. Willis Polk helped restore it in 1913, and it was again restored between 1990 and 1994.

There's a small fee to see the interior, the cemetery, and the museum, but it's worth it.

Masses are held regularly Monday through Saturday at 7:30 and 9am, and there's a Saturday vigil at 5pm; Sunday mass is at 8 and 10am in English and at noon in Spanish. But regardless of when you come, be sure to wander within the mission's 4-foot-thick walls and have a look at the wonderful painted and gilded altar and the incredible ceiling.

The ceiling and beams are done in an Ohlone Indian tribal pattern (one of the two main tribes of Native Americans who were the Bay Area's first inhabitants) and were painted with vegetable dyes. The altars and statues in the niches came directly from Mexico between 1800 and 1810.

Exit the church on the right side, just in front of the altar, and go left through the covered porch, where you'll find a series of photographs that show the mission at various stages in its history. Continue around and enter the small museum, which used to be the mission classroom but now holds various artifacts, including the baptismal register that dates from 1776, and some sacred items that were gifts of Father Serra. Note also the wood trusses; originally, they were held together by rawhide strips, but they were given steel reinforcements in 1918 as protection against earthquakes.

Exit the museum and you'll find yourself in a peacefully landscaped, fountained courtyard. You can sit here and relax if you like before entering the cemetery.

The cemetery dates from 1830. Seventy percent of those buried here are pioneer children; the second largest group is people of Irish descent. It's interesting to walk around the graveyard reading the epitaphs. Charles Cora, hanged by the Vigilante Committee of 1856, is buried here—look for the brown sandstone grave marker embellished with firemen's helmets. Another criminal hanged by the vigilantes, James P. Casey, also is buried in the cemetery. Dignitaries of the church are buried alongside the wall of the church. Among them is Francisco de Haro, the first mayor of San Francisco.

Go back around, through the courtyard and museum, to the covered porch. Follow the signs to the:

16. **Basilica of San Francisco,** which is the official parish church. The original building did not survive the

earthquake in 1906 and was rebuilt. This structure was completed in 1918.

Not every church has the honorable title "basilica," which can be conferred to a church only by the pope. In 1952, Pope Pius XII designated this building a basilica, and the red-and-gold umbrella and coat of arms with the papal insignia on the altar are symbols of the church's special status.

Although this church's interior is less exciting than the mission, it is interesting to note that the windows depict Saint Francis of Assisi (patron saint of the city) and the 21 California missions. Also of interest is the woodcarving of Mater Dolorosa, Our Lady of Sorrows, above the main altar, and the Seven Sorrows of Mary, which are visible above the door at the rear and on the side balconies.

Unless you already arranged transportation, you've got a long walk back to 24th and Mission. If you don't want to hoof it, you can catch the J Metro train heading south on Church; take it to 24th Street, then walk back to Mission. (Incidentally, the J also goes downtown, if that's where you're headed next.) Or better yet, follow 16th Street east toward Valencia. The blocks surrounding 16th and Valencia act as the hub of the Mission District's hip, alternative culture and contain plenty of cheap ethnic restaurants and eclectic shops. Here, too, you can catch the no. 26 bus heading south, which will let you off on 24th a few blocks west of Mission Street.

A Historical Flashback Through Haight-Ashbury

Start: Haight Street at Stanyan Street.

Public Transportation: Bus: 7, 33, 37, or 43.

Finish: Corner of Haight and Shrader streets.

Time: 1 to 3 hours.

Best Times: Between 11am and 6pm.

Worst Times: After dark.

Hills That Could Kill: None (though Buena Vista Park is a bit of a climb).

Although San Francisco already had a reputation as a liberal and colorful city, the goings-on in Haight-Ashbury (once known as the "Hashbury") during the late 1960s secured the city's status as the world's headquarters for counterculture. During the 3-year period surrounding 1967's "Summer of Love" (which actually amounted to well over a year), thousands of soul-searching youths migrated to this neighborhood to participate in a continuous impromptu street fair of nonviolent anarchy, free love, psychedelic drugs, and music. The movement was a spontaneous and profound rejection of the prevailing American Dream and the Vietnam War, and although there was community-wide animosity toward the status quo, no one could have anticipated the influence this small neighborhood would ultimately have on modern culture as a whole.

It was Haight Street's low-rent housing that first lured the young and artistic, but as the street's reputation grew, the alternative crowd expanded with it. At its height, thousands of hippies, artists, musicians, poets, lost souls, and philosophers danced barefoot through the streets, dressed in costume, ornamented with beads and feathers, or decorated with flowers in their hair. Free food was distributed to hundreds of homeless. The nearby Victorian apartments served as crash pads, meditation centers, art studios, band rehearsal and performance halls—and drug dens. Free concerts in Golden Gate Park drew thousands who came to celebrate their love for each other, their love for life, and their advocacy of peace. From the unified masses emerged such social icons as Allen Ginsberg, Timothy Leary, Janis Joplin, and The Grateful Dead.

By the end of the 1960s, the momentum slowed. Many social leaders moved out of the area to pursue careers, escape the law, or basically get on with life. Times were changing, but the Haight had already made an everlasting impression on the world as the place where it all went down.

Now, as you walk the neighborhood, you'll notice that Haight Street is capitalizing on its past notoriety. Toking hippies have been replaced by token souvenirs. The place is trendy enough to harbor a barrage of hip clothing and shoe stores, nostalgic enough to host a number of tie-dye T-shirt and smoke shops featuring every type of water pipe (bong) you could ever imagine, and funky enough to tolerate the leftover and new generation of hippies and homeless who beg for cash

Haight-Ashbury

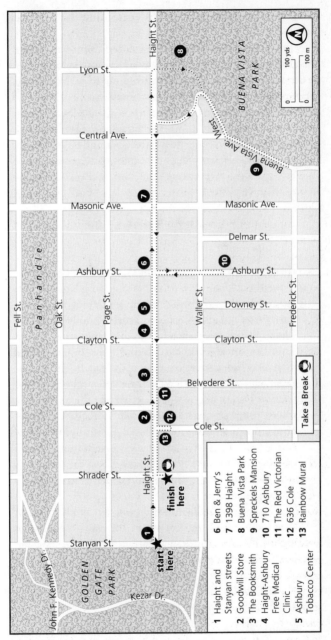

Haight St.

BUENA VISTA PARK

100 yds
100 m

Lyon St.

Central Ave.

Buena Vista Ave. West

Masonic Ave.

Masonic Ave.

Delmar St.

Ashbury St.

Ashbury St.

Page St.

Waller St.

Downey St.

Frederick St.

Clayton St.

Clayton St.

Belvedere St.

Cole St.

Cole St.

Fell St.

Oak St.

P a n h a n d l e

Shrader St.

Haight St.

finish here

Take a Break

Stanyan St.

start here

John F. Kennedy Dr.

GOLDEN GATE PARK

Kezar Dr.

1 Haight and Stanyan streets
2 Goodwill Store
3 The Booksmith
4 Haight-Ashbury Free Medical Clinic
5 Ashbury Tobacco Center
6 Ben & Jerry's
7 1398 Haight
8 Buena Vista Park
9 Spreckels Mansion
10 710 Ashbury
11 The Red Victorian
12 636 Cole
13 Rainbow Mural

from passing pedestrians. It's still a spectacle, for sure, but less genuine by far.

There are certain other things you can count on during a walk through the Haight: cheap, tasty food; cafe culture; wildly dressed youth; and plenty of activity mixed with beautiful, well-kept Victorian and Edwardian homes (some of the most desirable in the city, especially south of Haight St. in "Cole Valley"). In many ways, this densely packed area still embodies San Francisco's free spirit—a tolerance for every kind of lifestyle imaginable. Consider it a people zoo accentuated with interesting shops, architecture, and history, in which you're bound to enjoy a stroll.

• • • • • • • • • • • • • • • •

The first stop is at:

1. **Haight and Stanyan streets, northeast corner.** Until the end of 1997, the beginning of Golden Gate Park across the street was a makeshift camp of homeless— lots of young kids with tattoos, pierced body parts, and leather mixing with aging hippies and other street people. Truth is, some locals liked it that way: It proved San Francisco had a space for everybody. But in response to locals' concerns, Mayor Willie Brown fenced off the area under the guise of gussying it up, leaving the homeless to set up camp throughout the neighborhood's doorways, nooks, and crannies. (Surely that did not calm the locals' concerns.) Since then, the homeless have scattered; a new gateway to Golden Gate Park has been erected; and now a smaller group of squatters can be seen most mornings and afternoons.

Meanwhile, some locals still complain about problems that stem from drug dealing in the area (especially at night), but the homeless in this area generally have not been cause for alarm for locals or tourists.

Walk east, away from the park on Haight Street. Cross Shrader, and as you come to the intersection of Haight and Cole Street, notice the:

2. **Goodwill Store,** at 1700 Haight. When it was initially under construction in the early 1990s, it was slated to be

a Walgreens. But when the company paid no heed to public protest against the national chain opening on a sacred countercultural street, the building mysteriously burned to the ground halfway through construction. Anticonformists might be less obvious here now, but the concept is anything but dead.

Continue east on Haight to 1664 Haight St., home of:

3. **The Booksmith,** the neighborhood's best bookshop, with a few great reflections on Haight-Ashbury. For a quick overview, if the book is in stock, buy or flip through *The Summer of Love,* Gene Anthony's photo and text documentary about "Haight-Ashbury at its highest." This place is definitely a trip, in more ways than one.

Follow Haight farther, cross Clayton Street, and at the northeast corner, at 558–560 Clayton St., is the:

4. **Haight-Ashbury Free Medical Clinic,** which came into existence in 1967 in response to the community's obvious need for it. At the beginning, a substantial number of patients came here when they needed help coming down from LSD overdoses. Today the clinic's free services are available through a number of offices throughout the city. They offer everything from vaccinations and help for runaway homeless youth to drug-detoxification programs.

A short distance farther on Haight, you'll find the:

5. **Ashbury Tobacco Center,** 1524 Haight, which was said to be the "red house" referred to in the Jimi Hendrix song of the same name. You'll notice that today it's looking rather purple and notably commercial. Cashing in on the street's reputation, this new shop is chock-full of '60s-style paraphernalia: lava lamps, flasks, all kinds of cigarettes, metal stash boxes, pipes (including an incognito sort that's shaped like a lipstick), an extensive array of water pipes (which I've been told should not be referred to as "bongs" because the term implies intended illegal usage), lighters, and rolling papers.

As you come upon the corner of infamous Haight and Ashbury, you'll find:

6. **Ben & Jerry's,** 1480 Haight, the only big business that's been well received by the neighborhood. Its popularity

could be due to the company's politically progressive attitude, but more likely it's 'cuz they relate to the people with ice-cream names like Cherry Garcia and Wavy Gravy and a groovy staff. Take a look across the street, and you'll notice a Gap clothing store, which moved in some years ago to cash in on tourist business and has been locally protested since its opening. (Though a national chain, to be fair the company is based here in San Francisco.)

Keep on truckin' down Haight, cross Masonic, and you'll be in front of:

7. **1398 Haight,** which once was the infamous Drugstore Cafe. Built in 1903, this bygone neighborhood pharmacy eventually became a place to come for a lot more than just a couple of aspirin. Later, the storefront became the cafe Magnolia Thunderpussy's, and most recently, a restaurant/ brewpub called Magnolia Pub & Brewery.

Continue down Haight Street 2 blocks and you can't miss the grassy entrance to:

8. **Buena Vista Park.** Although some say this woodsy oasis has become a gay pickup spot, its splendid views and tall trees also make it a favorite for picnicking local residents. Notice that because the park's trees are planted at the bottom of the hill, as you climb, your viewpoint changes from being level with the base of the trees to being level with the treetops. It's also impossible not to notice the beautiful homes that surround the park's perimeters.

Exit on beautiful Buena Vista West, go left, uphill, and at 737 Buena Vista you'll find the:

9. **Spreckels Mansion.** One of the two mansions in the city built by the Spreckels family, who made their fortune from sugar (their other mansion, in Pacific Heights, is now the private home of romance novelist Danielle Steel; see Walking Tour 7, stop 6), this one was finished in 1887. It was once a B&B, with such notable boarders as Jack London and Ambrose Bierce. Today, however, it's a private home.

What a Long, Strange Trip It's Been

San Francisco's rock bands were a key element of the counterculture scene that blossomed in the city in the mid-1960s. Their free-form improvisation was one of the primary expressions of the hippies' "do your own thing" principle. Until 1995, you could still experience something of that scene by attending a concert by The Grateful Dead, the quintessential psychedelic rock band. Beneath the tie-dyed shirts and blissful smiles were a set of musical values that dated back to the days of Ken Kesey and his Merry Pranksters, a no-holds-barred tradition of spontaneous improvisation even at the expense of clarity.

The city was deeply saddened in August 1995 by the death of the band's leader, Jerry Garcia, one of San Francisco's cultural icons. Jerry played in a number of Bay Area bands before founding the Dead in 1965; but it was with the Dead that he gained real recognition and began headlining in local counterculture strongholds such as the late Bill Graham's Fillmore Theater. From June 1966 to the end of 1967, the Dead lived communally at 710 Ashbury St. and played numerous free concerts there. As 1967's Summer of Love brought the flower children into full bloom, the Dead set the tone for one enormous citywide house party, liberally seasoned with ample doses of marijuana and acid.

The Grateful Dead played together for nearly 30 years; if you ever caught one of their concerts, you got a small glimpse of Haight-Ashbury in 1967. Today, more than 7 years after Jerry's death, Dead memorabilia and recordings are still bestsellers in the small shops throughout the neighborhood, demonstrating that in this neighborhood's heart, and in the memories of millions, Jerry is still very much alive.

Continue up the hill to the intersection. Go right on Frederick Street then right on Ashbury Street. When you pass Waller, you will see:

10. **710 Ashbury,** a beautiful Victorian that served as The Grateful Dead's headquarters during the 1960s. There's no real indication of the Dead's past here. Nonetheless, the house itself and those around it are striking enough to admire regardless of whether you were a fan or not.

Go back to Haight Street and head west, past Clayton Street. Midway through the next block, at no. 1665, you can't miss:

11. **The Red Victorian.** Built in 1904 to accommodate visitors headed to the new Golden Gate Park (which was once just a small landscaped patch, with miles of sand dunes stretching all the way to Ocean Beach), this hotel endured the 1906 earthquake, but by the 1970s it was in need of some serious TLC. Owner and confessed former flower child Sami Sunchild bought it in 1977 and turned it into a "living museum" entirely dedicated to the Summer of Love and Golden Gate Park. Today, rooms are decorated accordingly—psychedelic posters, crochet, beads, and all. You probably won't be able to tour the rooms, but you can enter the Peace Center, where posters and colorful hippie-era signs are on display along with a soothing vibe and groovy gifts.

To counteract any sense of peace you might have achieved, head west and turn left on Cole Street. Halfway down the block you'll come upon:

12. **636 Cole,** where Charles Manson lived in the 1960s. The modest doorway shows no indication of its notorious previous tenant or his murderous past, but the thought of his having been here is still enough to give you the creeps.

On a cheerier note, head back to the corner of Haight and Cole. Cross the street to come upon the:

13. **Rainbow Mural,** which brightens up the wall just north of Haight on Cole Street. Artist Yana Zegri, who managed the building in 1967, painted the mural that year and still comes back here from Florida when it's in need of a

touch-up. It was renovated in 1981, 1983, and 1997 and portrays a fanciful depiction of evolution.

Hopefully you're a bit hungry by now, because you're about to come upon two great places to grab a bite. Turn left and follow Haight to the corner of Shrader:

Winding Down Decide whether you're in the mood for supercasual pizza or Mexican food, or more festive, heavier Caribbean food. **Escape From New York Pizza,** at 1737 Haight, offers counter service and classic New York–style slices. **Zona Rosa,** 1797 Haight, serves healthy and hearty burritos, and its window-front seating allows for front-row people-watching. Across the street at **Cha Cha Cha,** 1801 Haight, order some sangria, fried calamari, and a plate of mussels in saffron broth; you won't even care who's passing by outside.

Golden Gate Park: A Museum, Blooms & Trees from Dunes

Start: At the "Panhandle entrance" (the park's John F. Kennedy Dr.) and Stanyan Street.

Public Transportation: Bus: 7, 21, 33, or 71 will take you within 2 blocks of the starting point.

Finish: Either 9th Avenue and Lincoln Boulevard, or the Panhandle entrance.

Time: 3 to 4 hours, depending on how much time you spend in the park's various museums.

Best Time: Sunday, when the main drag of the park (John F. Kennedy Dr.) is closed to traffic between Kezar Drive and Transverse Drive.

Worst Times: None.

Hills That Could Kill: The climb to the top of Strawberry Hill (optional).

The onset of the gold rush forced San Francisco to grow quickly, and greed-driven real estate barons bought land so fast that no one had much time to think about reserving open spaces for the public. Not until the late 1860s did city officials realize the necessity for a sizable public park where residents could go to escape the bustle of San Francisco's increasingly crowded streets. Around 1870, they chose a piece of land located on the outer edge of what was then "the city" for the creation of a major park. Primarily composed of sand dunes, this parcel of land was 3 miles long and a half-mile wide. Apparently, it didn't occur to anyone that shaping a tract made of dunes and wind would present a serious challenge for a landscape artist.

In 1871, William Hammond Hall was appointed to the position of park superintendent. Hall worked for 5 years planning the park's layout, which included curved roads that accentuated a more rural environment and would encourage carriages to move slowly. He resigned in 1876, without having accomplished much more than that.

Not much changed for the next 11 years, but in 1887, John McLaren arrived on the scene. Once a student and gardener's helper at London's Royal Botanic Gardens, McLaren followed his heart to the temperate climate of San Francisco, where he could create beautiful gardens and plant thousands of trees.

Soon after he arrived in San Francisco, city officials hired him to landscape the park because he had just developed a new strain of grass called "sea bent," which held sandy soil in place. McLaren agreed to take on the project under four conditions. First, he needed $30,000 a year for planting. Second, he wanted as much water as necessary. Third, he requested that daily sweepings of horse manure from the streets be used as fertilizer. And fourth, there were to be no KEEP OFF THE GRASS signs.

They agreed but didn't really think he could accomplish the enormous task in front of him.

They laughed when McLaren built two windmills for pumping water at the park's ocean edge because they thought he was pumping saltwater. But he wasn't. They chuckled when he planted the "sea bent" and other seedlings because they thought the plants would never take root. But they did. They chuckled to themselves when the park designer planted rhododendrons, then they began to think he might be on to something.

He was. It took about 10 years before Golden Gate Park really began to take shape, and there was another problem to contend with—Ocean Beach's waves kept sweeping the far end of the garden out to sea. Slowly but surely, McLaren was able to solve that problem, too, by placing bundle after bundle of sticks on the beach so that each time the waves came up they would cover the sticks with sand. Each time the sticks were covered, he put more out, and together McLaren and the ocean built a wall between the waves and his park. It took 40 years, but today that wall is topped by the highway that runs along the ocean at the west end of the park.

Forty years is a long time to spend building a natural wall, but McLaren had the patience of a saint—except when it came to the statues that city officials insisted on placing all over his park. He called them "stookies," and he hated them. In fact, each time they put up a new one, he planted trees and shrubs and flowers to hide it. Even today, you'll notice that if you want to see the park's statues, you're going to have to hunt a little because, as McLaren intended, many are fairly well hidden.

In the 1890s, Golden Gate Park hosted the San Francisco Midwinter Exposition, and today you can still see some of the structures that remain from that world's fair, including the Japanese Tea Garden and the nearby band shelter at the Music Concourse.

John McLaren cared for the park for 50 years and was loved by all San Franciscans for his contribution to the city of his dreams. Today, his lifetime achievement offers something for everyone: an endless array of sunbathing spots, flower gardens, wooded paths, fields, and facilities for tennis, horseshoe tossing, fly-fishing, handball, horseback riding, and more. Its grassy expanses set the stage for free opera, Shakespeare, and comedy, as well as various local celebrations throughout the year (especially on weekends during summertime).

Golden Gate Park

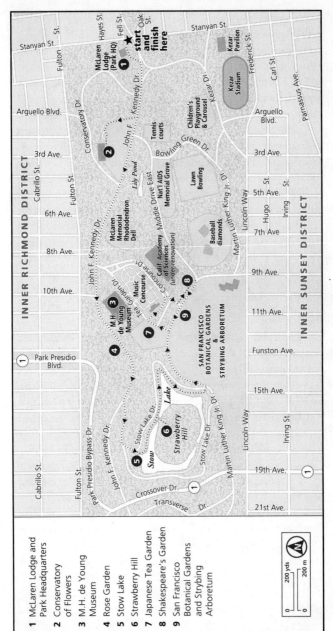

1 McLaren Lodge and Park Headquarters
2 Conservatory of Flowers
3 M.H. de Young Museum
4 Rose Garden
5 Stow Lake
6 Strawberry Hill
7 Japanese Tea Garden
8 Shakespeare's Garden
9 San Francisco Botanical Gardens and Strybing Arboretum

This walking tour will take you through part of one of San Francisco's greatest natural playgrounds, which includes numerous gardens, the stunning Conservatory of Flowers, a museum, and the man-made boating area called Stow Lake.

While planning your walk, keep in mind that the park lacks an excellent restaurant—except for the respectable cafe at the newly reopened de Young Museum. So consider packing a lunch. Alternatively, at the end of the tour, you can make your way to either 9th Avenue and Judah Street or Haight Street, where you'll find an abundance of excellent ethnic restaurants. Also note that there are endless worthy diversions from this tour, including plenty of intimate gardens and arboreal paths, so by no means follow this walking tour without exploring whatever catches your eye—and by all means, walk on the grass.

• • • • • • • • • • • • • • • •

As you stand at the northwest corner of Fell and Stanyan streets, walk into the park, and on your right the first thing you'll see is the:

1. **McLaren Lodge and Park Headquarters.** This building was the home of John McLaren from the time it was erected until his death in the early 1940s. You can pick up information here about this park (park maps are $3), as well as other parks and recreation areas in San Francisco; it's open Monday through Friday from 8am to 5pm.

If you're here during the holiday season, you won't be able to ignore the brightly lit tree out front, but children are especially awestruck by the lighting that outlines the lodge. Watch as it fades from one color to the next.

Go back to John F. Kennedy Drive and head right. The first lush, grassy expanse you'll see on your right generally caters to volleyball players. Farther along, Frisbee and sunbathing are the favorite pastimes for those who put down their picnic basket near the statue of Garfield.

Continue west. To your right, you can't miss the stunning, frosty-paned palace known as the:

2. **Conservatory of Flowers.** The conservatory was California's first municipal greenhouse, and it is the oldest building in the park. James Lick, the real estate baron, commissioned an Irish company to build this incredible glass house (patterned after the Conservatory Kew Gardens in England) and ship it to San Francisco. Completed in 1879, its design is indicative of late Victorian style.

The greenhouse itself is home to a remarkable collection of orchids and tropical plants. Unfortunately, due to age and harsh winter storms, visitors had not been able to enter the conservatory during the past several years. Thankfully, it underwent a $25-million renovation and is once again open to the public. The five galleries are abloom with enchanting botanical and horticultural displays.

Outside the conservatory sit an array of ever-changing, complex flower gardens that often depict pictorial scenes (after at least one victorious Super Bowl, the blossoms portrayed the 49ers' emblem!).

As you stand facing the conservatory, turn right and you'll come upon an old carriage turnaround that now harbors a glorious abundance of cacti on its periphery. In the center of the turnaround, be sure to admire the enormous blossoms of the wildly colorful dahlias (in bloom late spring to fall), which are Dr. Seuss–like in their size and shapes.

The conservatory is open Tuesday through Sunday from 9am to 5pm (last entry at 4:30pm). Admission to this tropical paradise is $5 for adults; $3 for youth ages 12 to 17, seniors, and students with ID; $1.50 for children ages 5 to 11; and free for children 4 and under. Admission is free to all visitors on the first Tuesday of every month.

Go back to John F. Kennedy Drive and turn right, heading west. As you walk along, you might want to make a few diversions on the arboreal pathways, which are invariably packed with flora and fauna.

If you're here on a Sunday, you won't be able to miss the roller-skating scene that takes place just before the Eighth Avenue exit from the park. Disco never died here, and the music and dancing are the same as they were in the late 1970s.

Continue on JFK Drive. Before you cross the concrete bridge on the right side of the street you'll see a modern copper-coated building on your left with a dramatic tower. Cross to the southern side of the street, and follow the road that leads to the building's entry. You'll be at the new:

3. **M. H. de Young Museum.** After being closed for a complete rebuild for a number of years, the de Young, which was founded in 1895, debuted its $190-million digs in October 2005. Though its fancy new design by Swiss firm Herzog & de Meuron and San Francisco's Fong & Chan Architects inspired controversy for its twisting tower, among other things, upon its reopening no one debated that what is now the world's largest copper-clad building is an exceptional museum. From the outside, the facility integrates art, architecture, and landscape with the intention of complementing and integrating with its surroundings. Inside is where you'll see the city's priceless American art collection, which spans the 17th to 20th centuries and includes art from America, Africa, and the Pacific. If you need to refuel, grab a table at the surprisingly good cafe. If you've got the time, the museum is definitely worth a visit and is open Tuesday through Sunday from 9:30am to 5pm (though it stays open until 8:45pm on Fri). Admission is $10 for adults, $7 for seniors, $6 for youth ages 13 to 17 and college students with ID, and free for children 12 and under. Also the first Tuesday of the month is free, and anyone with a Muni bus transfer gets $2 off.

Exit the museum the way you came in, go left and return to JFK Drive, then continue west. On the right side of the street you'll see the:

4. **Rose Garden.** Once you spot the garden, cross the street, and you'll find rows of bountiful blossoms (provided it's not winter). There's not a lot to do here, mind you, but this is one of the park's abundant opportunities to stop and smell some of life's simple pleasures.

Leave the Rose Garden via the route you came in. Make a right (west) back onto JFK Drive, and follow it until you find the little road called Stow Lake Drive, splitting off to the left. (You'll also see a log cabin in a small meadow beside the road.) Follow Stow Lake Road (about the length of a block) until it ends. You're now at the launching point for a peaceful pedal-boat or rowboat excursion or a pastoral stroll around:

5. **Stow Lake.** This is the biggest lake in the park, and although its water is an odd electric green, it's still one of the most tranquil respites from city life. Here, you'll find elderly Chinese citizens circling the lake for a bit of exercise, still-life painters, joggers, families, a content menagerie of resident ducks and turtles, and pedal boats for rent at Wheel Fun Rentals. Boats cost $17 per hour plus a $1 deposit, cash only. You can also rent mountain bikes ($8 per hour or $25 per day) and Surreys ($20 per hour). Walk clockwise around the lake, and you'll come upon one of two bridges that lead to a 430-foot-high, man-made island known as:

6. **Strawberry Hill.** Considering the tranquility that waits up top, it's surprising more people don't forge their way up here. Follow the well-marked stairways to one of the best vista points in the neighborhood, with bird's-eye views of the park and the bay beyond. Also be sure to stroll the islands' lake-level path, where you'll find the delightful Chinese Pavilion (a gift to the park from the city of Taipei) and a small, man-made waterfall.

To exit the lake area, return to the pathway surrounding the lake where you crossed the bridge. Continue clockwise until you see a path across the street at the horseshoe bend in the lake. Follow the sign down the stairs to the:

7. **Japanese Tea Garden,** which also was built for the temporary Midwinter Exhibition and would be one of the most peaceful places to pass the day were it not for the hordes of tourists and screaming children who pack into the gardens and the tea pagoda (especially during summer).

Despite the noise and its $3.50 entrance fee ($1.25 for children and seniors), it's a worthy excursion that's open daily from 8:30am to 6pm. As you walk among the bonsai and cherry trees, beside the flowers, and over bridges that cross pools of clear, still water, you can't help but feel at peace—especially when you come across the great bronze Buddha, which was cast in Japan in 1790 and donated to the park by the famous Gump family. (For more about the Gumps, see Walk 1, stop 12.)

You'll also come across a tiered, wooden shrine called the Shinto Pagoda and the steeply arched Wishing Bridge. If you look in the water below the bridge, you'll find that the bridge's reflection gives you the illusion that the bridge comes full circle.

For this wonderful Japanese oasis, we again have John McLaren to thank. In 1885, he had the wisdom to hire the Hagiwara family, which tended this jewel of a garden until they were sent to an internment camp during World War II. During their employment at the park, the Hagiwaras also supposedly either invented or introduced the fortune cookie in California (it's still served here in the pagoda, along with tea and a selection of rather unappealing packaged snacks). Much of the park is today named for the Hagiwara family.

After you visit the Tea Garden, I'd normally send you across the street to the enormous outdoor Music Concourse and science museum mecca, the California Academy of Sciences. However, they are under renovation—allegedly until 2008. But it's worth making a mental note for when they reopen. Why? Because, founded in 1853, it is not only the oldest scientific institution in the American West, it also happened to be a heck of a lot of fun to visit—and is bound to be even better when it reopens.

Within its confines will be newer versions of its original three attractions—the Steinhart Aquarium, the Natural History Museum, and the Morrison Planetarium. The aquarium houses a spectacular collection of fish, penguins, alligators, snakes, and tropical sharks.

But onward! Exit the tea garden, turning right. Walk about 150 feet to the main street (Martin Luther King, Jr., Dr., but there are no obvious signs). Turn left heading south until you see a sign for:

8. **Shakespeare's Garden,** where on plaques you can read lines such as

> Oh! had the monster seen those lily hands
> Tremble like aspen leaves, . . .
> He would not have touched them for his life.

> *(Titus Andronicus, II, 5)*

as you walk amid lilies, aspens, and the other flowers, herbs, brambles, and trees of Shakespeare's plays. The garden, founded in 1928, is usually a quaint, quiet spot to rest and enjoy the park. If by chance you're in love, try not to follow the example set by one of Shakespeare's characters:

> There is a man haunts the grove, that abuses our
> young plants with carving Rosalind on their barks;
> hangs odes upon hawthorns, and elegies upon
> brambles.

> *(As You Like It, III, 2)*

Unfortunately, noisy nearby construction might make this a less-than-romantic experience.

Exit the garden, turn left back to the street and head east. When you come to a "T" intersection, cross at the crosswalk and take the right fork. Before you know it, you'll be in front of the enormous and free:

9. **San Francisco Botanical Gardens and Strybing Arboretum.** Six thousand plant species grow here, among them some very ancient plants in a special "primitive garden," rare species, and a grove of California redwoods. You can tour the grounds yourself or take one of the docent-led tours available during operating hours— daily at 1:30 pm. Regardless, keep in mind that the gates are open Monday through Friday from 8am to 4:30pm and Saturday, Sunday, and holidays from 10am to 5pm.

From here, it's an easy stroll back to your starting point. Retrace your steps to the tea garden, but instead of going in, continue on the road until it merges into John F. Kennedy Drive. Merge with it and head right (east), following JFK Drive all the way back to the park headquarters. (If your feet have had it, you can exit the park by heading south, to the right, when exiting the arboretum. Up 1 block is the intersection of Ninth Ave. and Lincoln, where you can take the 16AX or 71 bus back to Stanyan St. Additionally, go 1 more block to Ninth and Judah sts. and you can catch the N Judah streetcar, which will take you all the way back downtown. Or just wander around the area and make yourself comfortable at one of the cafes.)

If you do walk back to your starting point, from here, you might want to turn right onto Stanyan and follow it to Haight Street, where, within the first 4 blocks, you'll find a profusion of cheap, delicious ethnic restaurants.

The Golden
Gate

Start: Fisherman's Wharf.

Public Transportation: Bus: 15, 19, 30, 32, or 39; Metro: F; cable car: Powell-Mason/Hyde Street line.

Finish: The Palace of Fine Arts, at Beach and Baker streets.

Time: 2½ to 4 hours, depending on your pace, whether you cross the Golden Gate Bridge, and how many stops you make along the way.

Best Times: After 10am when the shops and museums are open, when the weather's not too windy or damp, and when visibility is clear enough to see across Golden Gate.

Worst Times: Nighttime, extremely foggy and windy days, and before 10am.

Hills That Could Kill: The pathway leading from the Municipal Pier (it's not so bad) and the steps up to the Golden Gate Bridge.

Put on your walking shoes, grab a warm jacket, and put a new roll of film in your camera because you'll want to be well prepared for this tour, which explores San Francisco's coastal beauty with a dash of shopping, eating, drinking, museums, chocolate, piers, boats, and bridges along the way. Yes, it's a long one. But the historical treasures, man-made wonders, fresh air, wide-open space, and unobstructed and breathtaking views make this only-in-San-Francisco jaw-dropper of a jaunt one of my all-time favorites.

Few cities in America are as adept at wholesaling their historical sites as San Francisco, which has converted your starting point, Fisherman's Wharf, into one of the most popular tourist destinations in the world. Unless you come really early in the morning, you won't find any traces of the traditional waterfront life that once existed here; the only fishing going on around here is for tourist dollars.

Originally called Meigg's Wharf, this bustling strip of waterfront got its present moniker from generations of fishers who used to base their boats here. Today, a small fleet still operates from here, but basically Fisherman's Wharf has been converted into one long shopping mall stretching from Ghirardelli Square at the west end to PIER 39 at the east. Some people love it, others can't get far enough away from it, but most agree that Fisherman's Wharf, for better or for worse, has to be seen at least once in your life.

On the bright side, the bay-front scenes are spectacular, and it improves noticeably once you head toward Fort Point and the Golden Gate Bridge. Throughout much of your stroll along the water's edge, you'll have a postcard view of the bridge silhouetted by the rolling hills of the Marin Headlands. It's a serene dichotomy from the hustle and bustle of the wharf, a chance to see spandex-clad San Franciscans enjoying a post-war-era playground of converted military bases that are now part of the Golden Gate National Recreation Area.

As I mentioned, this walk is much longer than the other walks in this guide. But it offers such a wide variety of things to see and do: snack on seafood, vegetarian cuisine, and fresh and cheap Mexican fare; explore historic sailing ships; sip Irish coffees; watch the ships roll in; do a little shopping; visit the amazing Exploratorium—there's literally a full day's worth of

Northern San Francisco

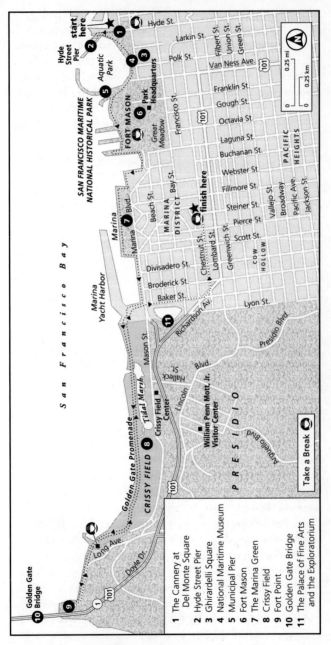

start here ★

Hyde St.

Larkin St.

Polk St.

Van Ness Ave. 101

Filbert St.

Union St.

Green St.

Hyde Street Pier

Aquatic Park

Park Headquarters

Franklin St.

Gough St.

Octavia St.

Laguna St.

Buchanan St.

Webster St.

Fillmore St.

Steiner St.

Pierce St.

Scott St.

Greenwich St.

finish here ★

Vallejo St.

Broadway

Pacific Ave.

Jackson St.

PACIFIC HEIGHTS

Francisco St.

Great Meadow

SAN FRANCISCO MARITIME NATIONAL HISTORICAL PARK

FORT MASON

MARINA DISTRICT

Beach St.

Bay St.

Marina Blvd.

Marina

Marina Yacht Harbor

Chestnut St.

Lombard St.

COW HOLLOW

Divisadero St.

Broderick St.

Baker St.

Lyon St.

Richardson Av.

Presidio Blvd.

San Francisco Bay

Golden Gate Promenade

Tidal Marsh

Mason St.

Halleck St.

Lincoln Blvd.

William Penn Mott, Jr. Visitor Center

PRESIDIO

Arguello Blvd.

Crissy Field Center

CRISSY FIELD

Long Ave.

Doyle Dr.

101

101

Golden Gate Bridge

Take a Break ⊙

1 The Cannery at Del Monte Square
2 Hyde Street Pier
3 Ghirardelli Square
4 National Maritime Museum
5 Municipal Pier
6 Fort Mason
7 The Marina Green
8 Crissy Field
9 Fort Point
10 Golden Gate Bridge
11 The Palace of Fine Arts and the Exploratorium

0   0.25 mi
0   0.25 km

adventure during this walk, so be sure to start early and bring a sweater for that chilly trip across the Golden Gate Bridge.

• • • • • • • • • • • • • • • •

We'll skip the tourist-tacky sections of Fisherman's Wharf (PIER 39, and so on—you know where it is if you want to see more). Head west on Jefferson Street until you arrive at:

1. **The Cannery at Del Monte Square.** This venerable three-story edifice was built in 1894 as a peach-canning plant for the Del Monte Fruit Company and converted in 1968 into a mall. The redbrick exterior was left intact, while the interior was transformed into a shopping and entertainment complex containing 50-plus shops, a paint-it-yourself ceramic studio, a comedy club, and several restaurants and galleries (including Jack's Cannery Bar, which features over 110 beers on tap).

   Across from The Cannery, at the corner of Jefferson and Hyde streets, is the entrance to the:

2. **Hyde Street Pier,** where you'll find several historic ships. Look for the *Balclutha,* a three-masted square-rigger that was built in Glasgow, Scotland, in 1886. It was used to carry grain and coal (among other things) from California and could travel at a near-record clip of 300 miles a day. In its lifetime, it rounded Cape Horn 17 times and even survived a near wreck off the coast of Alaska in 1906. During the last 30 years the *Balclutha* was in service, it made trips to Alaska for canned salmon. In 1934 the *Balclutha* played a minor role in the movie *Mutiny on the Bounty.* The ship is now completely restored. Visitors are invited to spin the wheel, squint at the compass, and imagine they're weathering a mighty storm. Kids can climb into the bunking quarters, visit the "slop chest" (galley to you, matey), and read the sea chanteys (clean ones only) that decorate the walls.

   The *C. A. Thayer,* a three-masted schooner built in 1895, was constructed for the lumber trade and carried logs from the Pacific Northwest to the many carpentry shops of California. It also served in two wars, and was the

Pacific Coast's last commercial sailing ship. Alas, if you drop by between now and 2008 or so you won't be able to see it. It's under restoration.

The *Eureka,* an 1890 paddle-wheel ferry that's been restored to its original splendor at the height of the ferry-boat era, made its final trip in 1957 (it was the last diesel-powered ferry to operate in the U.S.). It's a side-wheeler that used to carry automobiles as well as passengers, and if you go on deck, you'll find that it's loaded with a cargo of nostalgia that includes antique cars and trucks.

Other ships here include the two-masted *Alma,* one of the last scow schooners to bring hay to the horses of San Francisco; *Hercules,* a huge 1907 oceangoing steam tug; and *Eppleton Hall,* an English side-wheeled tugboat constructed in 1914 and originally meant to operate on the Thames River.

At the pier's small-boat shop, visitors can follow the restoration progress of historic boats from the museum's collection. It's located behind the maritime bookstore on your left as you approach the ships. Entrance to the pier is $5 for adults and free for children 17 and under. For more information, call ℂ **415/561-7100** or 415/447-5000 or visit www.maritime.org.

Take a brief but intoxicating diversion from the seaside stroll and hoof it up Hyde street (south, away from the water) to 2765 Hyde St., at the corner of Beach Street, where you should:

Take a Break Even if you're not an Irish-coffee fan, you can't help but get into the caffeine-and-whiskey spirit at The **Buena Vista** restaurant and bar. This ever-crowded spot not only makes San Francisco's best Irish coffees, it's also the first place in the United States to serve the uplifting combo of Irish whiskey, caffeine, and cream. Story has it that *San Francisco Chronicle* columnist Stan Delaplane tasted it in Shannon Airport and brought back the recipe in 1952. Along with Irish coffee, the cafe also serves casual fare like hamburgers and Rueben sandwiches, as well as a guaranteed good time with happy-go-lucky locals and visitors.

As you exit Buena Vista, turn left onto Beach Street, and on your right between Polk and Larkin streets is:

3. **Ghirardelli Square.** The massive brick complex dates from 1864 when it served as a factory making Civil War uniforms, but it's best known as the former chocolate-and-spice factory of founder Domingo Ghirardelli (say "*Gear*-a-deli").

Born in Rapallo, Italy, in 1817, as a boy he apprenticed himself to a confectioner. He later moved to Peru and opened his own candy shop. During his time there he had occasion to meet one of San Francisco's best, a man by the name of James Lick. Lick so enjoyed Ghirardelli's chocolate that he personally carried over 600 pounds of it back to San Francisco. In 1849, when Ghirardelli moved to San Francisco, he dazzled the taste buds of its residents, and while others were busy mining gold, he was making his fortune in chocolate. He later expanded his business to include the marketing of spices.

The 10-level shopping center you see today was the original Ghirardelli chocolate factory, built between 1900 and 1916. The sign that crowns the top has been there since it opened. The factory has been converted into a mall containing 50-plus stores and a couple dozen dining establishments. The stores generally stay open from 10am to 9pm in the summer and in winter they're open 10am to 6pm on weekdays and 10am to 7pm on weekends; the Information Booth has a detailed guide to the shops and restaurants. But in my opinion, the best reason to come is to visit the **Ghirardelli Chocolate Manufactory** (© 415/474-3938) soda fountain for a couple of scoops slathered in hot fudge. Incidentally, Ghirardelli Chocolate Company still makes chocolate, but it's located in a lower-rent district in the East Bay.

After you've finished jacking up your sugar level, cross the street, heading west on Beach. Continue until you come upon a white Art Deco building perched on the top of Victorian Park. This is the:

4. **National Maritime Museum.** Shaped like a ship with portholes and all, this free museum is filled with sailing,

whaling, and fishing lore. Remarkably good exhibits include intricate model craft (such as an exquisite model of the *Preussen,* the largest sailing vessel ever built), scrimshaw, and a collection of shipwreck photographs and historic marine scenes—including an 1851 snapshot of hundreds of abandoned ships, deserted en masse by crews dashing off to participate in the gold rush. The museum, which is free to the public and open daily from 10am to 5pm, also has walls lined with beautifully carved, brightly painted wooden figureheads from old windjammers.

When you exit the Maritime Museum, walk down through terraced Victorian Park to the pathway that runs along a small beach. This is the start of the 3½-mile paved **Golden Gate Promenade,** San Francisco's best and most scenic biking, jogging, and walking path, which leads all the way to Fort Point and the Golden Gate Bridge.

The long arm of a pier that you see stretching out before you is the:

5. **Municipal Pier,** where Van Ness Avenue dead-ends at the shore. This pier is a favorite for joggers, fishermen, and anyone who wants to take a short walk along a long pier in order to get gorgeous San Francisco views. If you're on a leisurely schedule, it's worth walking down to the very end and taking a look back at the city. Either way, you'll see Alcatraz—which protrudes from the bay just beyond the pier—and Aquatic Park, the safest spot to swim in the bay and the starting point for those brave and brawny few who swim to and from Alcatraz during local swim competitions. (If you've got loads of time, the San Francisco Maritime National Historical Park lies behind Aquatic Park, shaped like an Art Deco ship and filled with sailing, whaling, and fishing lore; 2 blocks east is Hyde Street Pier, where several historic ships are now moored and open to the public.) Also visible from here are the Golden Gate Bridge, the East Bay, Coit Tower, and downtown's skyscrapers—look for the pointy Transamerica Pyramid.

When you're done taking in the views, return to the base of the pier and head west (a left turn if you're facing the water). You will be facing the eastern entrance to:

Ominous Alcatraz

Visible from Fisherman's Wharf, Alcatraz Island (aka "The Rock") has seen a checkered history. It was discovered in 1775 by Juan Manuel Ayala, who named it after the many pelicans that nested on the island. From the 1850s to 1933, when the army vacated the island, it served as a military post protecting the bay shoreline. In 1934 the buildings of the military outpost were converted into a maximum-security prison. Given the sheer cliffs, treacherous tides and currents, and frigid temperatures of the waters, it was believed to be a totally escape-proof prison. Among the famous gangsters who were penned in cell blocks A through D were Al Capone; Robert Stroud, the so-called Birdman of Alcatraz (because he was an expert in ornithological diseases);

6. **Fort Mason.** There's much to see here, but first you'll need to walk up the entrance ramp and embark on a leisurely, beautiful walk through a park and the area known as The Great Meadow. Follow the paved path shaded by eucalyptus and Monterey cypress trees and scan the striking city skyline. When you come to the sign on the right side of the path that reads PIERS (there's an arrow pointing down a steep flight of steps toward the water), take those steps down to the bay-front buildings of Fort Mason. A former U.S. Army post dating back to the Civil War, the fort is now a national historic landmark. From the outside, its warehouselike facade is nothing to look at. But walk to Building A (the West Pier), the most western structure in the complex, and you'll find the **Museum of Craft & Folk Art** (✆ 415/775-0990), a great place to check out the latest exhibit and grab a unique gift or two, and **Greens Restaurant** (✆ 415/771-6222), the city's most famous vegetarian restaurant, overlooking boats bobbing in Yacht Harbor.

☕ **Take a Break** Even if you're not hungry, it's worth a peek at **Greens To-Go,** the restaurant's takeout counter. They serve coffee drinks and a delicious

Machine Gun Kelly; and Alvin Karpis. It cost a fortune to keep them imprisoned here because all supplies, including water, had to be shipped in. In 1963, after an apparent escape in which no bodies were recovered, the government closed the prison, and in 1972 it became part of the Golden Gate National Recreation Area. The wildlife that was driven away during the military and prison years has begun to return—the black-crested night heron and other seabirds are nesting here again—and a new trail has been built that passes through the island's nature areas. Tours, including an audio tour of the prison block and a slide show, are given by the park's rangers, who entertain their guests with interesting anecdotes.

variety of vegetarian sandwiches, salads, and desserts. If it's around lunchtime, consider sitting down in the straightforward dining room, where floor-to-ceiling bay-front windows star as the main visual attraction, and chef Annie Somerville's gourmet vegetarian cuisine leaves little reason to hanker for a hamburger.

When you're done exploring Fort Mason, head for the parking lot, staying to your right along the water, passing Yacht Harbor and leading to:

7. **The Marina Green.** This great stretch of grass is a favorite local playground. On any given day you'll see people jogging, flying kites, or playing a casual game of football. It's also an excellent place to relax on a bay-front bench and take in the scenic surroundings. When I'm here between late November and mid-February, I often sneak across the street to the Safeway supermarket (behind you), buy some fresh Dungeness crab (cooked and cracked), grab lots of napkins and deli packets of mayo and ketchup (mix 'em up), and fix a messy San Francisco–style snack right on the Green. If you don't have time for that, stay on course, walking along the

shoreline toward the Golden Gate Bridge and admiring the multimillion-dollar Mediterranean-style homes across the street. Given its appearance, popularity, and home and rental prices, you'd never know this neighborhood—known as The Marina—was the one hardest hit by the 1989 earthquake, since it was created on landfill for the Pan Pacific Exposition of 1915.

After a good 15-minute walk, you'll pass a small grass field and see a lone line of eucalyptus trees in front of you. Veer right just before the trees, following the sidewalk toward the bay. At the end of the road, you'll be standing in front of the water. To your left is the beginning of San Francisco's most beautiful recent addition, the recently restored marshlands known as:

8. **Crissy Field.** Since the surrounding area's restoration, it has become San Francisco's most prized strip of shoreline. Here you can spy coastal habitat, walk along a sandy, dog-friendly beach, watch windsurfers and kite surfers rip across the bay toward the Marin Headlands, and check out the city's most fashionable athletic-types as they trot along the pathway. As you continue toward the Golden Gate Bridge, you'll come across picnic tables and, just beyond, a giant shack where you can:

Take a Break The **Warming Hut** is nothing fancy, but it does crank out soul-warming teas and coffee drinks and offers decent sandwiches and great gifts themed with the Bay Area and its wildlife.

When you exit the Warming Hut, take a left turn, continuing on the bayside path headed toward the bridge. Soon you come upon:

9. **Fort Point,** a Civil War–era casement fort (the only one on the West Coast). This heavily fortified brick fortress was built in 1853 to protect the narrow entrance to the harbor. It was designed to house 500 soldiers manning 126 muzzle-loading cannons, and looks much the same today as it did when it was completed (though most cannons have been removed). By 1900, the fort's soldiers and obsolete guns had been removed, but the formidable brick edifice—with its 12-foot-thick walls—still remains.

Inside the fort there are exhibits on the first three of the four levels, including displays of armaments, the fort's hospital, and period artifacts and photographs. Today you can take a self-guided tour of the building, see bricks laid by laborers who worked for 50¢ per hour, eye ancient gunpowder barrels, or just hang out watching surfers as they shred the bone-chilling waters beneath the Golden Gate Bridge. *Take note:* The fort's only open Friday through Sunday from 10am to 5pm during Golden Gate Bridge retrofitting. For more information, call ℂ **415/ 556-1693** or visit www.nps.gov.

When you've had enough, retrace your steps back toward the Warming Hut. If you've still got energy, you can take a diversion up to the:

10. **Golden Gate Bridge.** Walk across it if you like, following the signs posted on your right and pointing you toward the stairs leading up to the southern end of the bridge. But even from afar, it's easy to admire this stunning San Francisco landmark. With its gracefully swung single span, spidery bracing cables, and zooming twin towers, the bridge looks more like a work of abstract art than one of the 20th century's greatest practical engineering feats. Construction began in May 1937 and was completed at the then-colossal cost of $35 million.

    The mile-long steel link (longer if you factor in the approach) reaches a height of 746 feet above the water, and is awesome to cross by foot, bike, or car. Millions of pedestrians walk or bike across it each year, gazing up at the tall red towers, out at the vistas of San Francisco and Marin County, and down into the stacks of oceangoing liners. You can walk out onto the span, but be prepared—it's usually windy and cold, and the bridge vibrates.

    Whether you take the bridge detour or not, you'll ultimately need to retrace your steps along Crissy Field and follow the path back the way you came. Once you arrive at the intersection of Mason Boulevard and Baker Street, turn right and cross Mason Boulevard. Follow Lyon toward the big domed building in front of you. At the intersection of Lyon and Palace Drive you'll find:

11. **The Palace of Fine Arts and the Exploratorium,** the only building left standing from the Panama-Pacific Exposition of 1915. Designed by Bernard Maybeck in a freely interpreted Roman style with romantic conception and Greek decorative treatments, it's one of San Francisco's most stunning structures, its beauty amplified by the surrounding park and lagoon—the perfect place for an afternoon picnic—and resident ducks, swans, seagulls, and grouchy geese.

If you're feeling playful and have money to spend, you can step inside the building and check out San Francisco's hands-on science museum, the **Exploratorium** (© **415/ 561-0356** for recorded information; www.exploratorium. edu). It contains more than 650 permanent exhibits that explore everything from giant bubble blowing to Einstein's theory of relativity—sort of like a mad scientist's penny arcade, educational fun house, and experimental laboratory all rolled into one. Here you can touch a tornado, shape a glowing electrical current, finger-paint using a computer, or pretend to dissect a cow's eyeball. Each exhibit at the Exploratorium is designed to be interactive, educational, safe, and, most important, fun. And don't think it's just for kids; parents inevitably end up being the most reluctant to leave. On the way out, be sure to stop by the gift store, which is chock-full of affordable brain candy and open from Tuesday through Sunday from 10am to 5pm and the occasional Monday.

Admission is $13 for adults, $10 for seniors and college students with ID, $10 for visitors with disabilities and youths 5 to 17, and free for children 4 and under. The museum is free for all the first Wednesday of each month.

Winding Down Surely you're tuckered out by now, and probably hungry. You can catch the no. 30 bus along Broderick Street (a block east), which will take you back to North Point Street and Van Ness, just 2 blocks south of Municipal Pier. Or head 3 blocks south, away from the bay, to Chestnut Street, turn left, and follow it to the beginning of that street's popular shopping and dining district. Here, the blocks between Divisadero and Fillmore streets are crammed with restaurants, clothing boutiques, juice and smoothie shops, home stores, and plenty of other reasons to part with your cash. A great cheap lunch can be had at 2150 Chestnut St., between Steiner and Pierce streets, where you'll find **Andalé Taqueria** (© **415/749-0506**). They serve tasty and fresh burritos, enchiladas, and mesquite-grilled meats at prices that tend to stay well below $10 for entrees.

From here, to get back to your starting point, you can retrace your steps along the waterfront or hop on the no. 30 bus at designated bus stops all along Chestnut Street. (Take a bus east of the Palace of Fine Arts; bus stops are on the south side of Chestnut St.)

Better yet, continue east on Chestnut; the section between Divisadero and Fillmore streets is considered one of San Francisco's premier shopping districts. Here you'll find a plethora of women's fashion boutiques; cafes; big-name chains like The Body Shop, The Gap, Williams-Sonoma, and Benefit; singles bars (only a scene after dark, mind you); and the city's yuppies meandering the area.

If you've exhausted all your retail therapy options and still have an urge to browse, take a right on Fillmore, follow it a few blocks up to Union Street. Turn left and you're in the epicenter of Pacific Heights' retail row. Look up the hills that dip down to Union and you'll see some of the city's most expensive real estate. Browse the shops and you'll find boutiques, home stores, and restaurants that cater to the city's well-to-do.

Essentials

This section includes all the basic information you will need to make your stay in San Francisco easier. There's a rundown of the layout of the city, plus transit information to make getting around a breeze. Finally, you'll find an A-to-Z list of basic information to answer virtually any question you might have.

VISITOR INFORMATION

Once in the city, visit the **San Francisco Visitor Information Center,** on the lower level of Hallidie Plaza, 900 Market St., at Powell Street (© **415/391-2000;** fax 415/362-7323; www.sf visitor.org), for information; brochures; discount coupons; and advice on restaurants, sights, and events in the city. They provide answers in German, Japanese, French, Italian, and Spanish, as well as English, of course. To find the office, descend the escalator at the cable car turnaround.

Dial © **415/283-0176** any time of day or night for a recorded message about current cultural, theater, music, sports, and other special events. This information also is available in German, French, Japanese, and Spanish.

Keep in mind that this service supports only members of the Convention & Visitors Bureau and is *very* tourist-oriented. Although there's a ton of information here, it's not representative of everything the city has to offer the off-the-beaten-track explorer. Still, the office is open Monday through Friday from 9am to 5pm, Saturday from 9am to 3pm, and Sunday—May through October only—from 9am to 3pm. It's closed on Thanksgiving Day, Christmas Day, and New Year's Day.

Pick up copies of the *San Francisco Bay Guardian* and *San Francisco Weekly.* The city's two free alternative papers list all city happenings—their kiosks and boxes are located throughout the city and in most coffee shops.

For specialized information on Chinatown's shops and services, and on the city's Chinese community in general, contact the **Chinese Chamber of Commerce,** 730 Sacramento St., San Francisco, CA 94108 (© **415/982-3000**), open Monday through Friday from 9am to 5pm.

The **California Welcome Center,** run by the Redwood Empire Association, at PIER 39, Suite Q5, San Francisco, CA 94133 (© **800/619-2125** or 415/292-5527; www.redwood empire.com), offers informative brochures and a very knowledgeable desk staff who are able to plan tours both in San Francisco and destinations north of the city. Their annual 48-page *Redwood Empire Visitors' Guide* (free via bulk mail) offers information on everything from San Francisco hotels, walking tours, and museums to visits to Northern California. The office is open daily from 10am to 7pm.

CITY LAYOUT

San Francisco's layout might seem confusing at first, but it quickly becomes easy to negotiate. The city's downtown streets are arranged in a simple grid pattern, with the exception of Market Street and Columbus Avenue, which cut across the grid at right angles to each other. Hills appear to distort this pattern, however, and can be disorienting. But as you learn your way around, these same hills will become your landmarks and reference points.

MAIN ARTERIES & STREETS **Market Street** is San Francisco's main thoroughfare. Most of the city's buses travel this route on their way to the Financial District from the outer neighborhoods to the west and south. The tall office buildings clustered downtown are at the northeast end of Market; 1 block beyond lie the Embarcadero and San Francisco Bay.

The **Embarcadero** curves along San Francisco Bay from south of the Bay Bridge to the northeast perimeter of the city and terminates at Fisherman's Wharf, the famous tourist-oriented pier. Aquatic Park and the Golden Gate National Recreation area are located farther on around the bay, occupying the northernmost point of the peninsula.

From the eastern perimeter of Fort Mason, **Van Ness Avenue** runs due south, back to Market Street.

The area described above forms a rough triangle, with Market Street as its southeastern boundary, the waterfront as its northern boundary, and Van Ness Avenue as its western boundary. Within this triangle lie most of the city's main tourist sights.

FINDING AN ADDRESS Because most of the city's streets are laid out in a grid pattern, finding an address is easy when you know the nearest cross street. When asking for directions, find out the nearest cross street and the neighborhood in which your destination is located, but be careful to not confuse numerical avenues with numerical streets. Numerical avenues (Third Ave., Fourth Ave., and so forth) are found in the Richmond and Sunset districts in the western part of the city. Numerical streets (Third St., Fourth St., and so forth) are south of Market in the eastern and southern parts of town.

GETTING AROUND

By Public Transportation

The **San Francisco Municipal Railway,** 949 Presidio Ave., better known as **Muni** (✆ **415/673-6864**), operates the city's cable cars, buses, and Metro streetcars. Together, these three public transportation services crisscross the entire city, making San Francisco fully accessible to everyone. Buses and Metro streetcars cost $1.50 for adults, 50¢ for youth ages 5 to 17, and 50¢ for seniors 65 and over. Cable cars cost $3 per person per ride ($1 for seniors 6–7am and 9pm–midnight) and are often packed with tourists. Exact change is required on all vehicles except cable cars. Fares quoted here are subject to change.

For detailed route information, phone Muni or consult the bus map at the front of the Yellow Pages. If you plan on making extensive use of public transportation, you might want to invest in a comprehensive route map ($2), sold at the San Francisco Visitor Information Center (see "Visitor Information," above) and in many downtown retail outlets.

Muni **discount passes,** called "Passports," entitle holders to unlimited rides on buses, Metro streetcars, and cable cars. A Passport costs $9 for 1 day, and $10 or $15 for 3 days or $20 for 7 consecutive days, respectively. Muni's **CityPass,** which costs $40 for adults and $31 for kids 5 to 17, entitles you to unlimited rides for 7 days and admission to the California Academy of Sciences, the Museum of Modern Art, the Exploratorium, Asian Art Museum, and Blue & Gold Fleet bay or Alcatraz cruises within 9 days of purchase. Among the places where you can purchase a discount pass are the San Francisco Visitor Information Center, the Holiday Inn Civic Center, and the TIX Bay Area booth at Union Square. To purchase tickets that include the Blue & Gold Fleet tour, call © **415/705-5555.** A $2.25 fee applies when using this phone service.

BY CABLE CAR San Francisco's cable cars might not be the most practical means of transport, but these rolling historic landmarks are a fun ride. There are only three lines in the city, and they're all concentrated in the downtown area. The most scenic and exciting is the **Powell-Hyde line,** which follows a zigzag route from the corner of Powell and Market streets, over both Nob Hill and Russian Hill, to a turntable at gaslit Victorian Square in front of Aquatic Park. The **Powell-Mason line** starts at the same intersection and climbs over Nob Hill before descending to Bay Street, just 3 blocks from Fisherman's Wharf. The least scenic is the **California Street line,** which begins at the foot of Market Street and runs a straight course through Chinatown and over Nob Hill to Van Ness Avenue. All riders must exit at the last stop and wait in line for the return trip. The cable car system operates from approximately 6:30am to 12:50am.

BY BUS   The Muni bus system extends to almost every corner of the city. It's not the most reliable system in the universe, but it works. Stops are designated by signs, curb markings, and yellow bands on adjacent utility poles; and most bus shelters exhibit Muni's transportation map and schedule. Many buses travel along Market Street or pass near Union Square and run from about 6am to midnight, after which there is an infrequent all-night "Owl" service. If you can help it, for safety purposes, avoid taking buses late at night.

Popular tourist routes are traveled by bus nos. 5, 7, or 71, all of which run to Golden Gate Park; 41 or 45, which travel along Union Street; and 30, which runs between Union Square and Ghirardelli Square.

BY METRO STREETCAR   Five of Muni's six Metro streetcar lines, designated J, K, L, M, or N, run underground downtown and along the street in outer neighborhoods. These sleek rail cars make the same stops as BART (see the following section) along Market Street, including Embarcadero Station (in the Financial District), Montgomery and Powell streets (both near Union Square), and the Civic Center (near City Hall). Past the Civic Center, the routes branch off in different directions: The J line will take you to Mission Dolores; the K, L, or M lines run to Castro Street; and the N line parallels Golden Gate Park and extends all the way to the Embarcadero. Metros run about every 15 minutes—more frequently during rush hours. Service is offered Monday through Friday from 5am to 12:45am, Saturday from 6am to 12:45am, and Sunday from 8am to 12:20am. The L or N lines operate 24 hours, 7 days a week.

Especially enjoyable to ride are the beautiful vintage multicolored F-Market streetcars, which run from downtown Market Street to the Castro and back. They offer a quick and charming way to get uptown and downtown without any hassle.

BY BART   BART, an acronym for **Bay Area Rapid Transit** (© **415/989-2278**), is a futuristic-looking, high-speed rail network that connects San Francisco with the East

Bay—Oakland, Richmond, Concord, and Fremont. Four stations are located along Market Street (see "By Metro Streetcar," above). Fares range from $1.25 to $7.45, depending on how far you go, though children 4 and under ride free. Tickets are dispensed from machines in the stations and are magnetically encoded with a dollar amount; computerized exits automatically deduct the correct fare. Trains run every 15 to 20 minutes, Monday through Friday from 4am to midnight, Saturday from 6am to midnight, and Sunday from 8am to midnight.

A $2.5-billion, 33-mile BART extension, opened in June 2003, includes a southern line that extends all the way to San Francisco International Airport.

By Taxi

This isn't New York, so don't expect a taxi to suddenly appear right when you need one. If you're downtown during rush hours or leaving from a major hotel, it won't be hard to hail a cab—just look for the lighted sign on the roof that indicates whether it is available. Otherwise, it's a good idea to call one of the following companies to arrange a ride: **Veteran's Cab** (© **415/552-1300**), **Luxor Cabs** (© **415/282-4141**), or **Yellow Cab** (© **415/626-2345**). Rates are approximately $2.85 for the first mile, and 45¢ for each fifth of a mile thereafter.

By Car

You don't need a car to explore downtown San Francisco, and in fact, in central areas such as Chinatown, Union Square, and the Financial District, a car can be your worst nightmare. (Let's not even get into hotel parking charges, which can cost up to $30 per day!) But if you want to venture outside the city, driving is the best way to go. Before heading outside the city, especially in winter, call to find out about California road conditions (© **800/427-7623**).

PARKING If you want to have a relaxing vacation, don't even attempt to find street parking in Nob Hill, North Beach, Chinatown, by Fisherman's Wharf, or on Telegraph Hill. Park in a garage, or take a cab or a bus. If you do find street parking, pay attention to street signs that explain when you can park and for how long. Be especially careful not to park in zones that are tow areas during rush hour.

Curb colors also indicate parking regulations. *Red* means no stopping or parking; *blue* is reserved for drivers with disabilities with a California-issued disabled plate or a placard; *white* means passenger loading and unloading only; *green* indicates a 10-minute limit; and *yellow* and *yellow-black* curbs are for commercial vehicles only (usually until 3pm). Also, don't park at a bus stop or in front of a fire hydrant, and watch out for street-cleaning signs. If you violate the law, you could get a hefty ticket, and your car might be towed.

When parking on a hill, apply the hand brake, put the car in gear, and *curb your wheels*—toward the curb when facing downhill, away from the curb when facing uphill. Curbing your wheels will not only prevent a possible "runaway," but also will keep you from getting a ticket—an expensive fine that is aggressively enforced.

The only days when most parking-meter limits are not enforced are New Year's Day, Thanksgiving Day, Christmas Day, Memorial Day, Independence Day, and Labor Day. However, you still need to feed the meters at Fisherman's Wharf during the last three holidays listed above.

DRIVING RULES   California law requires that all drivers and passengers wear seat belts. You may turn right at a red light (unless otherwise indicated) after yielding to traffic and pedestrians and after making a complete stop. Cable cars always have the right-of-way, as do pedestrians at intersections and crosswalks. Pay attention to signs and arrows on the streets and roadways, or you might find yourself suddenly in a lane that requires exiting or turning when you really want to go straight ahead. San Francisco's many one-way streets can also drive you in circles, though most road maps of the city indicate which direction traffic flows on these.

By Ferry

The **Golden Gate Ferry Service** fleet, Ferry Building (© **415/ 923-2000**), operates between the San Francisco Ferry Building, at the foot of Market Street, and downtown Sausalito (30 min.) and Larkspur (45 min.).

To/From Sausalito: Service to Sausalito is frequent, departing at reasonable intervals every day of the year except New Year's Day, Thanksgiving Day, and Christmas Day. Phone for exact schedule information. The ride takes half an hour and costs $6.15 for adults and $4.60 for kids 6 to 12. Seniors and passengers with disabilities ride for $3.05; up to two children under 6 with adults ride free on weekdays. Family rates are available on weekends.

To/From Larkspur: The Larkspur ferry is primarily a commuter service during the week, with frequent departures around the rush hours and limited service on weekends. Boats make the 13-mile trip in about 45 minutes and the one-way cost is $6.45 for adults, $4.85 for kids 6 to 12, and $3.20 for seniors and passengers with disabilities; on weekends, there is a family deal that includes two free rides for kids with each paying adult.

The Blue & Gold Fleet (recorded info: ℂ **415/773-1188;** www.blueandgoldfleet.com; tickets/operator: ℂ **415/705-5555**) operates daily from the Ferry Building and PIER 39 to Oakland, Alameda, and Vallejo. One-way fares are $7.50 for adults, $4.25 for children ages 5 to 11.

The Blue & Gold Fleet also operates shuttles from Pier 41 (Fisherman's Wharf) to Angel Island on a seasonal schedule.

FAST FACTS San Francisco

American Express For travel arrangements, traveler's checks, currency exchange, and other member services, American Express has an office at 455 Market St., at First Street (ℂ **415/536-2600**), in the Financial District, open Monday through Friday from 9am to 5:30pm and Saturday from 10am to 2pm. To report lost or stolen traveler's checks, call ℂ **800/221-7282.** For American Express Global Assist, call ℂ **800/554-2639.**

Area Code The area code for San Francisco and the peninsula is 415; Oakland, Berkeley, and much of the East Bay use the 510 or 925 area codes. The peninsula generally uses 650 and Napa and Sonoma counties are 707. All the phone numbers in this book are in San Francisco's 415 area code, but there's no need to dial it first if you're within the city limits.

Business Hours   Most banks are open Monday through Friday from 9am to 5pm. Many banks also feature ATMs for 24-hour banking.

Most stores are open Monday through Saturday from 10 or 11am to at least 6pm, with restricted hours on Sunday. But there are exceptions: Stores in Chinatown, Ghirardelli Square, and PIER 39 stay open much later during the tourist season; and large department stores, including Macy's and Nordstrom, keep late hours.

Most restaurants serve lunch from about 11:30am to 2:30pm and dinner from 5:30 to 10pm; sometimes you can get served later on weekends. Nightclubs and bars usually are open daily until 2am, when they are legally bound to stop serving alcohol.

Dentists   In the event of a dental emergency, see your hotel concierge or contact the **San Francisco Dental Office,** 131 Stuart St. (✆ **415/777-5115**), between Mission and Howard streets, which offers emergency service and comprehensive dental care Monday and Tuesday from 8am to 4:30pm, Wednesday and Thursday from 10:30am to 6:30pm, and Friday from 8am to 4:30pm.

Doctors   **Saint Francis Memorial Hospital,** 900 Hyde St., between Bush and Pine streets on Nob Hill (✆ **415/353-6000**), provides emergency service 24 hours a day; no appointment is necessary. The hospital also operates a **physician-referral service** (✆ **800/333-1355**).

Drugstores   **Walgreens** pharmacies are all over town, including one at 135 Powell St. (✆ **415/391-4433**). The store is open Monday through Friday from 7am to midnight, Saturday from 8am to midnight, Sunday from 9am to 10pm; the pharmacy is open Monday through Friday from 8am to 9pm, Saturday from 9am to 5pm, and is closed on Sunday. The branch on Divisadero Street at Lombard (✆ **415/931-6415**) has a 24-hour pharmacy.

Earthquakes   There will always be earthquakes in California, most of which you'll never notice. However, in case of a significant shaker, there are a few basic precautionary measures you should know. When you are inside a building, seek cover;

do not run outside. Stand under a doorway or against a wall and stay away from windows. If you exit a building after a substantial quake, use stairwells, not elevators. If you are in your car, pull over to the side of the road and stop—but not until you are away from bridges, overpasses, telephone poles, and power lines. Stay in your car. If you're out walking, stay outside and away from trees, power lines, and the sides of buildings. If you're in an area with tall buildings, find a doorway in which to stand.

Emergencies   Dial 𝄞 **911** for police, ambulance, or the fire department; no coins are needed from a public phone.

Liquor Laws   Liquor and grocery stores, as well as some drugstores, can sell packaged alcoholic beverages between 6am and 2am. Most restaurants, nightclubs, and bars are licensed to serve alcoholic beverages during the same hours. The legal age for purchase and consumption is 21; proof of age is required.

Newspapers & Magazines   The city's main daily newspaper the *San Francisco Chronicle* is available throughout the city. The Sunday edition includes a pink "Datebook" section, an excellent preview of the week's upcoming events. The city's free weeklies include the *San Francisco Bay Guardian* and *San Francisco Weekly,* tabloids of news and listings that are indispensable for nightlife information; they're widely distributed through streetcorner dispensers and at city cafes and restaurants.

Of the many free tourist-oriented publications, the most widely read are *Where, Key,* and *San Francisco Guide.* All three of these handbook-size weeklies contain maps and information on current events. They can be found in most hotels and in shops and restaurants in the major tourist areas.

Police   For emergencies, dial 𝄞 **911** from any phone; no coins are needed. For other matters, call 𝄞 **415/553-0123.**

Post Office   Dozens of post offices are located around the city. The closest to Union Square is inside Macy's department store, 170 O'Farrell St. (𝄞 **800/275-8777**). You can pick up mail addressed to you and marked "General Delivery" (Poste Restante) at the **Civic Center Post Office Box Unit,** General Delivery, San Francisco, CA 94142-9991 (𝄞 **800/275-8777**). The street address is 101 Hyde St.

Safety   Few locals would recommend that you walk alone late at night in certain areas, particularly the Tenderloin between Union Square and the Civic Center. Other areas where you should be particularly alert are the Mission District around 16th and Mission streets, the lower Fillmore area around lower Haight Street, Chinatown, and the SoMa area south of Market Street.

Smoking   If San Francisco is the state's most European city, the comparison stops here. Each year, smoking laws are becoming more and more strict. As of January 1, 1998, smoking was prohibited in restaurants and bars. With a few exceptions, the law is enforced in establishments. Hotels also are offering more nonsmoking rooms.

Taxes   An 8.5% sales tax is added at the register for all goods and services purchased in San Francisco. The city hotel tax is a hefty 14%. There is no airport tax.

Transit Information   The San Francisco Municipal Railway, better known as Muni, operates the city's cable cars, buses, and Metro streetcars. For information from a live person, call **Muni** at ⓒ **415/673-6864** weekdays between 7am and 5pm or weekends between 9am and 5pm. At other times, recorded information is available at the same phone number.

Guided Walking Tours of San Francisco

Just in case you have walked all of the tours in this book and are raring for more, I've included a list of great guided walking tours to San Francisco's most colorful districts. Yes, you have to pay for these, but they're probably the best deals you're going to get for your tourist buck: You'll meet new people, learn loads about the city, drink plenty of great coffee (and dine a la local-style as well, should you choose), and—best of all—you won't get lost.

NORTH BEACH

Javawalk is a 2-hour coffee/walking tour by self-described "coffeehouse wizard" Elaine Sosa. It's loosely a coffee and walking tour through North Beach, but there's a lot more going on than drinking cups of brew. Javawalk also serves up a good dose of historical and architectural trivia, offering something for everyone. The best part of the tour might be the camaraderie that develops among the tour goers; Sosa keeps the tour interactive and fun as she dispenses tales and trivia about the history of coffee and its

North Beach connections. It's a guaranteed good time, particularly if you're addicted to caffeine.

Javawalk is offered Saturday at 10am and Sunday through Friday for private parties of 6 or more by appointment only. The price is $20 per person, half price for kids 12 and under. For information and reservations, call Elaine at © **415/673-WALK** (9255) or visit javawalk.com.

CASTRO

Cruisin' the Castro is an informative historical tour of San Francisco's most famous gay quarter, giving a totally new insight into the contribution of the gay community to the political maturity, growth, and beauty of San Francisco. Tours are personally conducted by Trevor Hailey, who was involved in the development of the Castro in the 1970s, and who personally knew Harvey Milk, the first openly gay politician elected to office in the United States. You'll learn about Milk's rise from shopkeeper to city supervisor, and visit Harvey Milk Plaza, where most of the city's gay and lesbian marches, rallies, and protests begin. In addition, you'll explore the Castro Theatre; adjacent side streets lined with beautifully restored Victorians; and a plethora of community-oriented stores in the Castro—gift shops, bookstores, restaurants, jewelers—whose owners Hailey knows personally.

The tours are conducted May through November Tuesday through Saturday from 10am to 2pm, beginning at Harvey Milk Plaza atop the Castro Street Muni station. The cost includes lunch at a local restaurant. Reservations are required and can be made by calling © **415/550-8110** or online at www.webcastro.com/castrotour. The tour, with lunch, costs $45 for adults, $40 for seniors 62 and over; the cost is flexible for children depending on their age.

HAIGHT-ASHBURY

Nostalgic for the 1960s? Then the **Haight-Ashbury Walking Tour** is for you. The 2½-hour tour revisits old hippie haunts such as The Grateful Dead's crash pad, Janis Joplin's house, and other reminders of the Summer of Love. Yes, Virginia, if it happened in the '60s, it all happened here: the Human Be-in, the Digger feeds, the free concerts, the Love Pageant Rally, and much more. You will rediscover the neighborhood's forgotten history, including the often-overlooked Victorian architecture and remnants of the Haight's former life as a resort. But wait, there's more! You'll also receive loads of insider advice on the area's best bars, restaurants, and hip shops, as well as the latest gossip about this tie-dyed cradle of hippie culture.

The walking tour, operated by Pam and Bruce Brennan (longtime Haight-Ashbury residents), begins at 9:30am Tuesday and Saturday. The cost is $15 per person, cash only, but BYOBuds. Reservations are required. For information and reservations, call ✆ **415/863-1621.**

CHINATOWN

San Francisco's Chinatown is always fascinating, but for many visitors with limited time, it's hard to know where to find the "nontouristy" shops, restaurants, and historical spots in this microcosm of Chinese culture. **Wok Wiz Chinatown Walking Tours & Cooking Center,** founded more than a decade ago by author, TV personality, cooking instructor, and restaurant critic Shirley Fong-Torres, is the answer. The Wok Wiz tours take you into nooks and crannies not usually seen by tourists. Most of her guides are Chinese, speak fluent Cantonese or Mandarin, and are intimately acquainted with all of Chinatown's alleys and small enterprises, as well as Chinatown's history, folklore, culture, and food.

Tours are conducted daily from 10am to 1:30pm and include dim sum (Chinese lunch). It's an easy, fun, and fascinating walk, and you're bound to make new friends. Groups generally are held to a maximum of 15, and reservations are essential. Prices (including lunch) are $40 for adults, $35 for seniors 60 and over and children under 12; without lunch, prices are $28 and $23, respectively.

Shirley Fong-Torres also operates an **I Can't Believe I Ate My Way Through Chinatown** tour that starts with a Chinese breakfast in a noodle house, moves to a wok shop, and then makes further stops for nibbles at a vegetarian restaurant, rice noodle factory, and a supermarket before taking a break for a sumptuous luncheon (most Sat; $75 per person, including the meal). And for all you gourmet cooks, there's Shirley's **Walk & Wok** tour, which includes shopping for food in Chinatown and then cooking—and eating—it together at Shirley's Cooking Center (most Sat; $100 per person).

Reservations are required for all tours and can be made by calling ✆ **650/355-9657** (www.wokwiz.com).

ALCATRAZ

If you haven't already taken a tour of The Rock, I strongly urge you to do so—it's one of the best guided tours I've ever been on. The tour starts at Pier 41 at Fisherman's Wharf, where you board a ferry that takes you to the island. From there, you're escorted into the bowels of the former prison, where you're shown an informative slide show given by the park's rangers (who entertain their guests with interesting anecdotes), followed by a superb guided audio tour of the prison block that incorporates the voices and stories of actual former inmates and guards.

Because of the popularity of the tour and limited space, we recommend that you purchase tickets as far in advance as possible. The tour is operated by **Blue & Gold Fleet** (✆ **415/705-5555;** to buy tickets online go to www.telesails.com) and can be charged to a credit card (American Express, MasterCard, Visa; $2.25 per ticket service charge on phone orders). Tickets ($12 adults, $9.75 seniors 62 and over, $11 children 5–11) also can be purchased in advance from the Blue & Gold ticket office on Pier 41, but advanced purchase is required because tours sell out. Ferries depart every 15 and 45 minutes after the hour. Operating hours are summer daily from 9:30am to 4:15pm, and winter daily from 9:30am to 2:15pm. Night tours (Awesome! Eerie!) depart Thursday through Sunday at 4:20 and 5:10pm. Arrive at least 20 minutes before sailing time, and take a heavy sweater or windbreaker because even when the sun's out, it's cold. Also remember that there are a lot of steps to climb on the tour, so wear the proper shoes. For recorded ticket and tour information, call ✆ **415/773-1188.**

VICTORIAN HOME TOUR

Jay Gifford, founder of **Victorian Home Walk Historical Walking Tour** and a San Francisco resident for 2 decades, brings his enthusiasm and love of San Francisco to this highly entertaining walking tour. The 2½-hour tour, set at a very leisurely pace, incorporates a wealth of interesting knowledge about San Francisco's Victorian architecture, as well as the city's storied history—particularly the periods just before and after the great earthquake and fire of 1906. You'll stroll through the neighborhoods of Japantown (where you can take a break to cruise the trendy shops on Fillmore St.), and onward to Pacific Heights and Cow Hollow. In the process, you'll see more than 200 meticulously restored Victorians, including the one where the Hollywood film *Mrs. Doubtfire* was filmed. Jay's guests often find they are the only ones on the quiet neighborhood streets, where tour buses are forbidden—a big difference from the hustle and bustle of busy Union Square. The trip ends with a trolley bus ride back to Union Square, passing though North Beach and Chinatown on the way.

These tours, which start at Union Square at 11am, are offered daily and cost $20 per person. Reservations are required; call Jay at © **415/252-9485,** or visit his website at www.victorianwalk.com.

Index

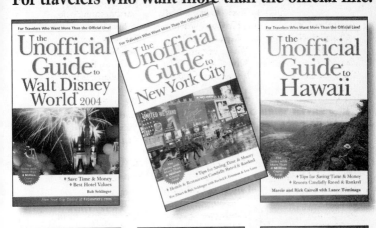

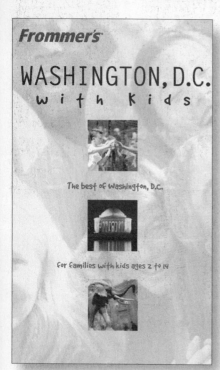

FROMMER'S® COMPLETE TRAVEL GUIDES

FROMMER'S® DOLLAR-A-DAY GUIDES

FROMMER'S® PORTABLE GUIDES

FROMMER'S® CRUISE GUIDES